5 EASY STEPS TO YOUR FIRST RENTAL PROPERTY

REAL ESTATE INVESTING GUIDE FOR BEGINNERS

E.J. WILLIAMS, U.S. ARMY VETERAN

© Copyright 2021 Blackstone Street Publishing LLC - All rights reserved.

It is not legal to reproduce, duplicate, or transmit any part of this document in either electronic means or in printed format. Recording of this publication is strictly prohibited and any storage of this document is not allowed unless with written permission from the publisher except for the use of brief quotations in a book review.

Under no circumstances will any blame or legal responsibility be held against the publisher, or author, for any damages, reparation, or monetary loss due to the information contained within this book. Either directly or indirectly. You are responsible for your own choices, actions, and results.

Legal Notice:

This book is copyright protected. This book is only for personal use. You cannot amend, distribute, sell, use, quote or paraphrase any part, or the content within this book, without the consent of the author or publisher.

Disclaimer Notice:

Please note the information contained within this document is for educational and entertainment purposes only. All effort has been executed to present accurate, up to date, and reliable, complete information. No warranties of any kind are declared or implied. Readers acknowledge that the author is not engaging in the rendering of legal, financial, medical or professional advice. The content within this book has been derived from various sources. Please consult a licensed professional before attempting any techniques outlined in this book.

By reading this document, the reader agrees that under no circumstances is the author responsible for any losses, direct or indirect, which are incurred as a result of the use of the information contained within this document, including, but not limited to, — errors, omissions, or inaccuracies

CONTENTS

Introduction	v
1. Understanding the Limiting Beliefs that Can Stop You from Getting Your First Rental Property	1
2. Funding Options	11
3. Find the Right Property	39
4. Find a Property Manager	51
5. Close on the Property	65
6. After Closing Details	81
7. Partnership Opportunity With a Team of Seasoned Real Estate Investors	99
Conclusion	103
Notes	109

MY GIFT TO YOU!!

Get your Free Property Analysis spreadsheet. This tool will help you figure out if the property is right for you. **What are you waiting for?!!** Start calculating your return on investment (ROI) **Right Now!!**

**Free Rental Analysis:
www.EJWilliamsInvesting.com**

INTRODUCTION

Did you know that 79 percent of millionaires are self-made and that many of them come from poor families? I bet you didn't know this!

According to research in *The National Study of Millionaires* by Ramsey Solutions, these 79 percent never had an inheritance, nor did they have huge salaries. All they had was a goal to become financially free, and they worked on that plan.

I come from a military family, so it wasn't surprising when I joined the US Army after high school. While serving in the Army, I got my first injury in 2010 and two years later; I was honorably discharged. Since I had only a high school diploma with an artillery background, the only jobs I could get were security and warehouse jobs.

Also, because of my injury, I went from job to job, so investing in anything at the time just seemed so unrealistic to me. My wife was pregnant with our second son and we lived in a one-bedroom apartment with barely enough to eat. Each time we went through our coin jars just to buy bread, peanut butter, and jelly, sadness would wash over me seeing my family living like that. I felt alone and helpless.

Things continued like this for another two to three years until I finally

INTRODUCTION

dared to dive into real estate investing. My mentor and a few friends were already in the business as real estate brokers, so it was easy for me to get guidance and dive into it. I knew I needed to have a financial plan, mainly because of my wife and three sons. I was also tired of my low five-figure income and my inability to secure a better-paying job because of my injury.

It took me years to realize my limiting beliefs had stopped me from investing early in real estate. Once I found a mentor to help me overcome those limiting beliefs, I could turn my low five-figure income into six figures in two years using residential real estate investing. If I hadn't found my mentor, who knows what would have become of me and my family?

You might relate to my story because you have been in a similar situation or you know someone who has. Whatever the case might be, gaining early financial freedom is not impossible. I also understand some limiting factors have stopped you from mapping out a plan for your financial freedom and they could be any of the following:

1. You have seen your poor background, age, poor salary, unemployment, and financial responsibility or debts as a limitation. There's this mental block that makes you think you can't be financially free when you have any or all of the problems above.
2. You don't have the knowledge, courage, or motivation to take action. The fear of the unknown kicks in and it stops you from achieving your goal of being financially free.
3. You don't have the time to wait for your investment to pay off since you want a get-rich-quick scheme where you earn money in the quickest time possible without doing much work. Or because your job, family, and having a busy life overall makes investing in real estate seem far-fetched.
4. You have bought books on real estate investing that were not being clear, had outdated information, and no call to action

INTRODUCTION

that could lead you in the right direction and spur you into starting your first investment in real estate.
5. Maybe the reason you haven't invested in real estate is that you have the interest but don't know how to get the funds to invest. You could be a college student or a veteran who doesn't have thousands of dollars in the bank waiting to be invested.

These are valid, and I understand what it means to have doubts about something. Trust me, if I didn't have my mentors and those few friends who were gracious enough to guide me into my first real estate investment, I wouldn't have taken that leap of faith and invested the little money I had.

I wrote this book from my knowledge and experience in real estate because I am passionate about sharing what I know. I am positive the contents of this book will help you, just as it has helped many others who have partnered with me in getting their first real estate investment. There is so much potential in real estate investment, and I want you to partake of this bounty.

Reading this book will benefit you in the following ways:

- You will get the courage you need to invest in real estate, you will become fearless and have faith. I will also demystify real estate investing and help destroy the limiting beliefs that have blocked you from living the life you deserve: a financially free life.
- You will be able to get your first rental property.
- You will be able to get into real estate on your own with this self-help guide, and you will learn how to partner with others to grow your real estate portfolio quicker. More so, if you choose to partner with other real estate investors, it will take less time, less effort, and give you a high return on investments (ROI).

With 11 years of experience in buying properties, rehabbing the prop-

INTRODUCTION

erty, being a landlord, and using equity strategies to increase ROI (Return on Investment), I can show you the exact things I did that have helped me become financially free. I have also learned the Dos and Don'ts of real estate from my business partner and mentor who has done over a billion dollars in deals.

If you are:

- A military veteran who needs a mission or a plan that will help you become financially free. As a veteran myself, I know how many veterans struggle to find their place in society after serving their country. So, I want to help my Battles find another purpose in their lives; something they can live for through gaining financial freedom.
- A college student who worries about finding work so that you can pay for your education. With a real estate investment, you can fund your education, earn passive income, and even have a place to live with the mortgage being paid by your tenant.
- Someone with 401K, IRA, Roth, traditional savings, or equity in the home, you can prepare for early retirement through real estate investing. There are so many people out there who have made it to the retirement age and do not have enough finances to retire, so they keep working. Many people are also old or have health problems and cannot do a lot of hands-on jobs. With this book, I will show you how to employ people or services that will take away the tedious part of real estate investing from your shoulders.

In **5 Easy Steps to Your First Rental Property** you will learn:

1. The limiting beliefs that can stop you from getting your first rental property and how to overcome them.
2. The different ways to get funding for your first rental property.
3. The property searching strategies will help you find the right property at a great deal.

INTRODUCTION

4. How to find the right property manager that will ease off the stress off you and help you manage the financial aspects of the property.
5. What to do and expect during closing a property.
6. The after-closing details will help you get your first rental property up and running.
7. About a partnership opportunity with my mentor, Kris Khron, and me with our team of seasoned real estate investors with a track record of 20 percent and above ROI (return on investment).

Are you ready to gain financial independence through investing in rental properties? Then dive in as I show you five easy steps to your first rental property.

1

UNDERSTANDING THE LIMITING BELIEFS THAT CAN STOP YOU FROM GETTING YOUR FIRST RENTAL PROPERTY

Growing up, I was told the story of a dog that was chained to a tree, and a bowl of food was placed in front of it by its owner. On seeing the bowl of food, the dog would reach for it, but the chain would pull it back. The dog tried several times to reach for the bowl of food, but it couldn't. The owner of the dog would later come and feed the dog himself thus, making the dog rely on him for survival. He continued to do this for months until he eventually set the dog free. Since this dog was used to being tied and not being able to reach its food by itself, even when it was set free, it didn't reach for the food in front of it.

Although the chain was no longer restricting this dog from getting its food, it still sat there hungry and didn't move an inch. This may seem weird but many people out there are currently living like this dog and the reason is that there is a mental block. They see opportunities to live a better life but do not go for it even when there are no barriers. So what they do is come up with one excuse after the other to justify why they can't achieve their goals. Like the dog in this story, their limitations exist only in their minds. These limitations that exist in the mind are called *limiting beliefs*. And, what makes it worse is, many people are not even aware that they hold these beliefs, neither do they know how to overcome them.

Limiting beliefs are defined as (also called self-limiting beliefs) are false or illogical thoughts that prevent people from pursuing or achieving their goals and dreams even when they can do these things. These beliefs can stop you from doing even mundane things like trying a new ice cream flavor. For me, I don't enjoy trying new dishes or flavors because I feel it will never end well. I got stuck with the mindset when, after a few times of trying new dishes and flavors, it didn't go well. But the funny thing is, there are other times I have been *pushed* to try new dishes, and it went exceptionally well. As I stated earlier, limiting beliefs start and end in the mind. They are nothing more than false beliefs about you, your situation, or the world.

Our beliefs also put limitations on what we consider reasonable behavior. For instance, I believe lying is wrong and so it stops me from telling any type of lie. Since we think limiting beliefs are all bad, some aren't. An example is a limiting belief I have about telling lies. Therefore, we need some limiting beliefs to help us check our behavior and stop us from doing the wrong things. However, some limiting beliefs stop us from becoming who we should become, and from doing what we should do to lead better lives. Just like the dog in my story that remains tied to the tree, these limiting beliefs keep many people in one place and they don't even know it.

Many people put off investing in real estate for years because it seems difficult to do. Even when they know the great benefits of investing in real estate and how vital it is to help change their lives and financial status. The reasons would-be investors do not see investing in real estate as an opportunity worth trying is because of limiting beliefs.

Limiting beliefs come in three forms:

1. Limiting beliefs about oneself: These are beliefs that make people feel they cannot achieve their goals or do anything worthwhile because something is wrong with them. Many

limiting beliefs about ourselves are rooted in emotional attachments and insecurities. Examples of limiting beliefs about oneself include age, traits or physical attributes, and emotions.

2. Limiting beliefs about the world: These are beliefs that make people think they cannot achieve anything because the world or other people are against them. Examples of limiting beliefs about the world include disapproval, sexism, racism, discrimination, many phobias, and religious bigotry. Some people even think they are so different from others that no one understands them, and because of this, they believe nobody will support their dreams.
3. Limiting beliefs about life: These are beliefs that make people think they cannot achieve their goals because it is too difficult. Some limiting beliefs in this category include people thinking they have missed out on an opportunity because they didn't start early or because other people are already doing what they want to do.

Limiting beliefs are mostly formed from childhood as we watch patterns in our family, school, and environment. These patterns then form the beliefs we would later have. As we get older, we form more complex beliefs from a wider range of sources like books, music, movies, television advertisements, our peers, etc. The core beliefs that we formed as young children are powerful, and even when we get new information or explanations about what we believe in, we still hold on to our old beliefs.

An example would be a young boy whose parents are hard workers and, as a result, are rarely present. This boy may form the belief that he isn't good enough, that's why his parents are never with him. However, later in life, he may come to the understanding that his parents worked hard because they loved and wanted to provide for him, which made their absence inevitable. But even as an adult, that early belief may be so deeply rooted in his mind that he continues to hold on to it.

Limiting beliefs are also one reason we don't like being wrong or corrected. Once we have formed a belief, we then look for more evidence to support that belief and discard contradictory evidence. This also means that beliefs can be difficult to get rid of, even when they are holding us back.

Examples of Some Limiting Beliefs

1. Making your health and happiness a priority is selfish.
2. If something seems healthy, it most definitely will not be enjoyable. You understand that health and happiness do not have to be opposites; they can work together.
3. Never change a plan. This is one common but sad limiting belief that has crippled many people. It is okay to have a constant goal, but it is not okay to stick to a plan when it isn't working. There are many ways to achieve a goal and if one isn't working anymore, discard it and use the next plan.
4. It is all or nothing! This belief is common amongst perfectionists who believe nothing should be imperfect otherwise why bother with it.
5. People beat themselves up when the things they think should be easy to turn out hard.
6. Talking about money or finances means you're greedy.
7. Happiness can only come when you are rich, popular, or have what you have always wanted.
8. Comparing yourself with others and seeing everyone as competition, etc.

Causes of Limiting Beliefs

Listed are some causes of limiting beliefs.

- Family.
- Education.

- Experiences (good or bad).
- Society or environment.
- Media (including social media).
- Religion.
- Culture.
- Overthinking the possibility of achieving a goal, etc.

How to Identify the Limiting Beliefs You Have

As I stated earlier, some limiting beliefs are subconscious and you may not even know you have them, yet they stop you from achieving your goals or going for what you want. Also, it is a known fact that before you can get rid of a problem; Identify it and know the cause of that problem.

Below are some strategies that will help you identify the limiting beliefs you have.

1. Carry out a blame-free analysis: Keep any reason you might have to blame yourself aside and analyze why you can't or couldn't achieve a goal. Ask yourself questions like, *"Were/ Are my goals realistic? Was the reason I didn't meet my goals external, internal, or a combination of both? What prevents me from taking action?"* Write the answers to these questions without blaming or judging yourself. You can group the results into health, business, finances, relationship, spiritual, etc. This will help you know the limiting beliefs you have without beating yourself up.
2. Take a trip to memory lane: As I stated earlier, many of the limiting beliefs we have were formed in our childhood and so it is only reasonable that we go back to trace those patterns that describe our upbringing. Writing answers to questions like, *"What were my parents/ guardian(s) like? What values did they have and bring me up with? How was the environment I grew*

up in? What were the people there like?" will help you figure this out.
3. Merge both answers: Compare the two answers you have above and draw out similarities. Look at the childhood beliefs you have and how they affect your current attitude or way of life.
4. Identify areas of recurring challenges: If there is a particular aspect of your life where you keep facing problems, this might be a pointer that a limiting belief you have is what has kept you in that situation for long. For example, if you spend more than you save and you are always broke, the reason could be because you believe your salary is too small to provide for your basic needs, much less, save.

PS: You might also need the help of a therapist, especially if you had a traumatic childhood, and reliving your memories become hurtful. It is wiser to get a therapist to help you identify the limiting beliefs you have instead of trying to do it on your own.

How to Overcome Limiting Beliefs

One thing you must understand is beliefs are not facts and they may be helpful or not. But the truth remains that the beliefs we have shaped how we think and behave. However, we must learn to overcome those limiting beliefs that hold us back from achieving our goals.

Below are some ways to overcome limiting beliefs in life and in investing in real estate.

1. Consider the possibility of being wrong: Whenever a belief you have is challenged instead of defending it (which I know will be hard not to do), try to keep an open mind and listen to what the other person has to say. Since you believe that what you know is right, the truth is your belief is not a fact and you might be wrong. Being open to correction is a way you can get rid of the limiting beliefs you have. Even if nobody challenges

your beliefs, ask yourself what if you are wrong and what if none of the things you have held onto for so long are relevant?
2. Ask if you are gaining anything from having that belief: Most times, people hold on to beliefs that serve them. For example, someone who feels they are so different from every other person in the world, or they are too old to go after their dreams might use this to garner self-pity or empathy from others. And because of this attention they get, they choose to hold on to their beliefs even when it is not serving them positively.
3. Set a firm deadline: If the reason you haven't invested in real estate through rental properties is that you don't have the time, a solution to this problem would set an investment deadline for yourself. Since lack of time has become a limitation, it is only wise that you do not give yourself room for procrastination.
4. Hire a property manager: You must have heard the saying that no man is an island. The same is true when investing in real estate, especially if you are a newbie and venturing into the business without ample time on your hands. Many reputable companies can help you hire a great property manager who will see to the affairs of your rental property. So not having enough time or knowing what to do shouldn't be an excuse for you anymore, as you can simply hire a property manager to help you.
5. Find funding options: I have mentioned earlier that lack of money is one of the biggest reasons many people shy away from getting their first rental property. But the funny thing is, many people who have invested in real estate did not use their own money. Crazy, right? I will explain more of this in the next chapter, but what is important is that you open your mind to see the possibility of investing in real estate, even if you have nothing saved up or no friends or relatives to lend you some money.
6. Stop overanalyzing and get right into it: People who over analyze and overthink before taking action often miss out on

great opportunities. Now, it is not wrong to analyze or sleep on a matter before deciding however, when your analysis points out everything that could go wrong, then you know it is time to stop. Nothing in this world is guaranteed a favorable end; not your life, job, relationship, or business, but you do them anyway with the faith that it will work. So, apply this same mindset and start making moves to get your first rental property.

7. Form new beliefs: In trying to get rid of old limiting beliefs, form new ones that are healthy and will push you to achieve your goals. For each of the stifling negative beliefs, you have identified, form a new one to replace it.
8. Work on your mind and mindset again: Though the brain can hold on to beliefs, it can still be retrained to let go of old beliefs and adopt new ones. There are many ways you can do this. You could try writing or speaking your new beliefs repeatedly at specific times every day, or start new habits or rituals to support the new belief e.g. make a small, intentional mistake if you are battling perfectionism.
9. Look for inspiration from people or places that can help sustain your new mindset: Look for people in business or other areas of life that portray the new beliefs you now have. Once you have identified people to follow, read books by them or about them, study how they achieved success and the struggles they had to overcome. Also, put up inspirational quotes and images that suit the limiting belief you are trying to get rid of where you will regularly see them.

With investing in real estate, the major limiting belief people have is the lack of money. Another limiting belief is the lack of time to follow up the investment process. Now that you have understood the limiting beliefs that have held you back from owning your first property and how to overcome them, we are already halfway in the journey to helping you get your first rental property.

The next steps you will need to take to achieve this set goal of owning your first rental property are:

- Step One: Funding Options.
- Step Two: Find the Right Property.
- Step Three: Find a Property Manager.
- Step Four: Close on the Property.
- Step Five: After Closing Details.
- Step Six: Get Guidance from our Team of Seasoned Real Estate Investors.

Each of these steps will be thoroughly explained as individual chapters of this book, to guide you in a step-by-step manner for getting your first rental property.

Chapter Summary

In summary:

1. Limiting beliefs are defined as (also called self-limiting beliefs) are false or illogical thoughts that prevent people from pursuing or achieving their goals and dreams even when they can do these things. These beliefs can stop you from doing even mundane things like trying a new ice cream flavor.
2. One thing you must understand is beliefs are not facts and they may be helpful or not. But the truth remains that the beliefs we have shaped how we think and behave.
3. With investing in real estate, the major limiting belief people have is the lack of money. Another limiting belief is the lack of time to follow up the investment process.
4. In the next chapter, you will learn about funding options.

2

FUNDING OPTIONS

Now that you have understood what limiting beliefs are and how to overcome them so you can get your first rental property and prepare for financial freedom, the first step is to find funding options.

But before then, we need to get some basic definitions across for better understanding, as they will also be used a lot in this book.

Rental property is a home or property bought by an investor who then puts it up for lease to tenants or other types of rental agreements and makes revenue from it. Depending on the state of the rental property, an investor might need to rehab or do some work (fixer-upper) on the property before giving it to a tenant. However, the property you buy should have only minor repairs and not major ones, so you don't run into a loss.

Funding is the act of providing the resources to finance a need or project. It could be provided by the government, an organization or group of people, or an individual. Funding can also be a grant or a loan and there are different sources of funding, namely:

1. Personal savings.
2. Family and friends.
3. Crowdfunding.
4. Angel investors.
5. Venture capital.
6. Bank loans.
7. Small Business Administration (SBA) loans.

There are many advantages to investing in real estate, including the fact that the monthly revenue gotten from a rental property increases when there is inflation. Also, unlike the stock market, real estate investment is not volatile. However, to get started with investing in real estate, you need some money. Whether this money is yours, it doesn't matter.

What's important is that you have some money to invest in getting your first rental property.

In this chapter, I will narrow down the funding options to four options, namely:

1. Loan options
2. Partnering options.
3. Hard money lender options.
4. 401K, IRA, whole-life insurance, and TSP (Thrift Savings Plan).

Loan Options: A loan is a sum of money that is expected to be paid back with interest. Before a loan is given, both parties (the lender and borrower) would have a set of terms that they agree to which will guide paying back the loan. In this loan option for funding your first rental property, I will show you seven of the best loan investment options you can choose from, what property they are best used for, the requirements, their current interest rates and APR (Annual Percentage Rate), the loan size minimums and maximums, the length and complexity of the underwriting process (which involves the lender checking the borrower's credit history, assets, size of the loan request, debt, etc before the loan is approved).

An **investment property loan** is money given to an investor to buy or build a property that has the potential to generate income either through leasing or re-selling that property.

Seven of the Best Investment Property Loan Options
1

1. **Best Overall:** Quicken Loans
2. **Best for Veterans:** Veterans United Home Loans
3. **Best for Single-Family Homes:** Citibank
4. **Best for Commercial Property:** Lendio
5. **Best for Low Down Loans:** Northpointe Bank
6. **Best for Ground-Up Construction:** Nationwide Home Loans Group, a division of Magnolia Bank
7. **Best for Rehab Loans:** LendingOne

Quicken Loans[2]: I chose *Quicken loans* as the best overall investment property lender because they lend nationwide, offer a wide variety of loan types, and make applying for a mortgage online very easy for the borrower which is awesome as you don't need to walk into an office to get a loan. You can simply apply from the comfort of your home. Quicken also gives competitive rates, which helps solidify its position as the best overall mortgage lender.

Quicken Loans was formed as a physical lender in 1985 and moved online in 2000. It is safe to say it rose parallel to the growth of the internet. They also offer a large portfolio of loan products that can be tailored to an investor's needs when they complete their online application. Quicken loans lend on **residential and multi-unit investment properties** with fixed and adjustable-rate home loans, mortgage refinancing, FHA, USDA, and VA loans, and jumbo loans (which is a type of loan that exceeds the limit set by the Federal Housing Finance Agency) for higher-priced homes.

On conventional loans, Quicken offers down payments as low as 3 percent if an investor qualifies for their agency loans. If an investor doesn't qualify, they should plan on putting 20 percent of the loan amount down if their credit score is below 700, and potentially 15 percent down if their credit score is above 720. The current mortgage rates for a 30-Year Fixed loan carry a rate of 3.62 percent and an APR of 3.86 percent. For their 15-Year Fixed loan product, the rate is 2.75 percent with an APR of 3.21 percent.

Note that an investor can only get these rates and down payment percentages on up to four investment properties limited to single-family homes or multifamily properties up to four units. After they hit that mark, they will need to turn to get alternate financings such as private equity and private or hard money lenders. These lenders often require 30 percent down, and rates are 3 percent to 6 percent higher.

The loan minimum for Quicken loans depends on the type of property, but the loan maximum is up to $2 million for their jumbo loan program. Rocket Mortgage now acts as the online platform and loan processor for Quicken Loans. Rocket can check employment, income, and financial assets by accessing direct deposit information provided by 98 percent of U.S. financial institutions. If you are not paid by direct deposit, income and employment information can be verified for about 60 percent of working Americans through Rocket's access to various databases. This allows for faster processing and a 30-day time frame to close.

Advantages:

- The availability of online applications and live agents to talk to.
- Instant verification of employment and income for over 60% of working Americans.

- Custom fixed-rate loan terms that are between eight and 30 years.
- They offer agency loans with a 3% down payment.

Disadvantages:

- Quicken loans don't offer home equity loans or HELOCs (Home Equity Line of Credit is a line of credit secured by your home, which is a revolving source of funds like credit cards).
- There are no branches to visit in person.
- They do not consider alternative credit data, only credit scores, and debt-to-income ratio.

Veterans United Home Loans[3]: This is my best investment property lender **for veterans** because the firm specializes in VA-backed mortgages with experts who understand this loan program (and their specific consumer base) better than anyone else. It was founded in 2002 and is a full-service lender that specializes in VA loans for qualifying veterans, active service members, and their spouses. They are one of the biggest VA mortgage lenders in terms of volume in the United States.

With this loan option, investors benefit from flexible qualification guidelines, lower rates, and monthly payments, no down payments, and no private mortgage insurance. Veterans United has VA loans for as little as 0 percent down, and they understand how to make the VA loan work for an investor and remain within the program's guidelines.

For a VA loan to be used on an investment property purchase, it must be a **multifamily property no larger than four units**, and the investor must live in one unit. This is a key point, and if they don't meet this criterion, the VA loan cannot be used for an investment property. But if they follow this rule, they will benefit from the low down payment and low rate benefits this government program provides. Among the products offered are fixed and adjustable-rate mortgages, jumbo loans, refinance loans, and cash-out loans. **Loan rates** change daily, ranging from

2.250 percent to 3.5 percent with APRs between 2.8 percent and 3.5 percent.

Veterans United Home Loans **do not have a minimum loan amount declared.** If the investor is using a VA loan, the VA only guarantees up to the county-specific loan limit. For most counties, the limit is $548,250, but for some high-cost areas, the limit reaches $822,375. They also underwrite your loan by analyzing your credit score, debt-to-income ratio, cash reserves, and income, and they review the property inspection reports, appraisal, and title search results. This whole process could take between four to six weeks. However, most of the initial pre-approval stage is done online.

For investors to use a VA loan for their investment property, some documents they will be asked to provide are a copy of your driver's license or other government identification, a copy of your DD-214 or Reserve/Guard points statements, a statement of service for active duty borrowers, recent pay stubs and W-2s for the last two years, recent bank statements, and disability award letters.

Advantages:

- Offers 24/7 customer service over the phone.
- Has online application and pre-qualification.
- Employs advisors from each branch of the armed forces.

Disadvantages:

- Doesn't offer home equity loans or HELOCs.
- Information on FHA, USDA, and conventional loans is harder to find on its website
- They charge higher rates and fees than some other lenders.

Citibank[4]: This is my best choice for investment property lenders for **single-family homes** because it offers a full toolbox of home loan products for investors, more low down payment options than other lenders, and some of the lowest rates and fees in the industry. CitiBank was founded in New York in 1811 and it provides a suite of tools that investors can use for different strategies to finance their single-family home income properties. The bank has fixed-rate mortgages for 10, 15, 20, and 30 years, and 3/1, 5/1, 7/1, and 10/1 adjustable-rate mortgages.

Their conventional loans lend up to $548,250 in many countries and up to $822,375 in some high-cost areas. Above those prices, Citibank can meet an investor's needs with a jumbo loan. This lending option mirrors the VA loan and has terms up to 30 years with rates comparable to conventional mortgage interest rates. **Loan minimums** are determined on a case-by-case basis, but they normally range between $50,000 and $75,000. Citibank underwrites residential, multi-unit, and commercial properties.

Existing Citibank customers benefit from closing cost credits and rate discounts, but they must set up automatic monthly mortgage payments from their Citibank deposit account. The **rates change daily** with the current interest rates ranging from 2.375 percent to 3.125 percent, with APRs from 2.722 percent to 3.33 percent. Investors can qualify for these rates as long as they have not exceeded four mortgages, which is the limit set by Fannie Mae (Federal National Mortgage Association).

For an investor's fifth investment property purchase, they could combine their first four properties into a single blanket loan, where they get to make one mortgage payment applied to the debt on all four properties combined. This way, they would become eligible for yet another low-interest loan. If an investor does not merge the mortgages, they will have to turn to private and hard money lenders where the rates are 3 to 6 percent higher, with prepayment penalties, and require down payments as high as 30 to 35 percent.

The **underwriting process** takes between 30 to 60 days. An investor can begin their Citibank mortgage application over the phone, online, or in-person depending on the location. If an investor starts online, they can be connected with a loan officer for pre-approval.

. . .

Advantages:

- They offer a wide variety of loan options.
- They provide customizable mortgage rates on their website.
- Low rates and fees compared to other lenders.
- Low down payment HomeRun program.

Disadvantages:

- They charge a mortgage application fee.
- Requires help from a mortgage loan officer to complete the loan application online.

Lendio[5]: This is my most preferred for **commercial property loans** because their marketplace platform is the simplest way an investor can fill out one application and receive offers from multiple competing lenders. Lendio is a free online service for investors, where they receive potential commercial loan offers within minutes from the company's marketplace of over 75 lenders. Over 216,000 loans have been funded through Lendio, thus giving it an excellent reputation for success. Unlike other commercial property options, they make the process simple with one application to shop rates.

Lendio lenders underwrite residential, multi-unit, and commercial real estate loans, including an array of business loans too. Down payments can be as low as 3 percent if an investor qualifies for one of the agency loans, like FHA. Otherwise, traditional commercial property loan programs require 25 percent to 30 percent down. **Interest rates** start at 4.25 percent on the Lendio platform for commercial property loans. The terms range from 20 to 25 years and take a minimum of 45 days to fund. Commercial property loan amounts range from $250,000 to $5 million.

Lendio suggests that investors should have the purchase contract, property blueprints, market analysis for the property, project budget and scope of work, and assessment of the property's existing conditions ready for an organized underwriting experience. The online application takes about 15 minutes and is where it all starts, and documents are shared electronically once an investor has selected a lender.

Advantages:

- It is a 15-minute application process.
- It offers a wide range of financing options and lenders.
- It has personalized guidance and expertise to help investors interpret their loan offers.

Disadvantages:

- There is a high-interest rate on some loans.
- Hard credit inquiry.
- An investor has to fill out their online application before they can see the loan terms.

NorthPointe Bank[6]: Northpointe Bank is great for its low down loans because it offers an impressive level of convenience along with its multiple loan options, including several with 100% financing. For the past six years, Independent Community Bankers of America (ICBA) has ranked Northpointe Bank as one of the top-performing banks in the nation out of a field of approximately 5,500 ICBA member banks.

Northpointe Bank has *three loan programs* that do not ask for a down payment, making it our top choice if you are an investor seeking a low down payment investment loan. The *EquityBuilder program* has a $0 down payment, no monthly insurance, flexible loan terms, and a maximum loan amount of $750,000. It is also a *VA lender*. With a VA loan, there is no-down-payment program, an investor can finance single-family, multi-unit, and condos. However, this VA loan can only be used on a primary residence, so if you buy a multi-unit property as an investment, you need to live in one unit (same as the Veterans United Home Loans). Their third option for a loan that requires no down payment is their *Doctor loan* for rehabs. These loans can be used for a purchase or refinance and lend up to $1.3 million, and mortgage insurance is not required.

Rates change daily: the current interest rates range from 2.6 percent to 3.75 percent and APRs between 2.7 percent and 3.8 percent. Interested investors will have to fill out the *Find an Advisor* form on its website. Then the loan advisor will contact the investor and get the needed information. For faster transactions, investors are expected to prepare documents such as pay stubs and bank statements.

Advantages:

- A full slate of loan offerings.
- Offers a no-down-payment loan with a shorter repayment term.
- A mobile app for customer convenience.
- Serves all 50 states plus Washington, D.C.

Disadvantage:

- Only one ARM product (five-year).

Nationwide Home Loans Group[7]: It is a division of Magnolia Bank, an independent community bank founded in Kentucky in 1919. The bank has grown its services to lend nationwide and generates over $1 billion in home loans annually. Nationwide Home Loans Group is the best construction lender for investors because it merges up to three loans into one closing process, lends in most states, and has loan officers available seven days a week. Its programs offer the lowest down payment requirements for a ground-up construction loan, and no payments are due during construction.

This construction loan is the best because it has a combination of features that no other lender has put together into one program for a **single-family residential investment**. An investor can buy land, build the house, and finance the mortgage, all with one closing process. Also during the construction period, investors enjoy enhanced liquidity because they don't have to make any payments until the home is finished.

Their construction loan size minimum is $125,000, and their maximums mirror the Fannie Mae and Freddie Mac loan (Federal National Mortgage Association & Federal Home Mortgage Corporation) limits which are determined by county. For most counties, the loan maximum is $548,250. Interest rates fluctuate based on the market, but Nationwide's interest and APR rates range from 1 to 1.25 percent, which is more than traditional mortgages for a pre-built home. No mortgage payments are collected until the construction is complete.

For **underwriting**, the lender requires the borrower's median of three credit scores to be at least 640. An investor will make initial contact online, but the rest of the process is done through email and phone as they exchange documents with their loan processor. Besides providing a personal financial statement, the investor needs to submit building plans and information about their builder's credentials. The loan officer will walk them through exactly what they need, depending on the specific details of their project.

Down payments vary depending on the particular loan program. For example, their VA construction loan can be as low as 0 percent down, and their FHA loan can be as low as 3.5 percent down. Give it a space of two weeks to rate-lock, and closing will happen before construction starts. At the end of the construction period, which is typically around six months, the loan automatically converts to a long-term mortgage with no second closing.

Advantages:

- Investors can get up to 100% financing.
- Loan officers are available seven days per week.
- They lend nationwide.
- They can finance land purchase, construction loan, and permanent mortgage into one rate-locked closing.

Disadvantages:

- One combined loan could translate into higher rates on the final permanent mortgage.
- Investors must have 640 as their minimum credit score.
- Full documentation lender.

LendingOne[8]: It is the best rehab lender because they are one of the very few commercial lenders that make it easy to get a pre-approval letter, they finance up to 90 percent loan-to-cost and provide lower rates and fees than their competition. LendingOne was founded in 2014 by Bill Green and Matthew Neisser because of their frustrations with the difficult lending environment from rigid bank criteria and the easier, but more expensive option, hard money alternatives.

As a direct private real estate lender, LendingOne has become the best **rehab lender** in the industry because they help investors get pre-approval letters and proof of funds, higher leverage, and lower rates and fees. It offers fix-and-flip and rehab-to-rent loan products. **Down payments** range from 10 to 20 percent. Their 30-year loan for rehab-to-rent projects starts at 4.99 percent for the interest rate, with APRs slightly over 5 percent currently. Their fix-and-flip loans start at 7.49 percent, with APRs starting in the mid-8 percent range. Rates are based on credit score and loan to value (LTV). LendingOne loans on two- to four-unit properties only, including condos and townhouses.

The **loan minimum** is $75,000, and they will lend up to $2 million. Interest rates and loan terms are underwritten based on your experience, income, credit, and LTV. Their fees are transparent, too. Their loan origination fee ranges from 1.75 to 3 percent and closing costs are typically 2 to 5 percent of the loan amount. If an investor's credit score is in the low 600s, they will work with them based on the rest of their financial picture.

The **underwriting requirements** for the investor is to have six months of cash reserves, a recent bank statement, a list of properties they already own, a certification that they are buying the property for business or investment purposes, the operating agreement for their business entity, driver's license, purchase and sale contract, and a lease agreement if the property already has a tenant in place.

LendingOne can give rehab loans in as little as 10 days, and investors can apply online or over the phone.

PS: Underwriting is the process whereby financial institutions such as banks, insurance companies, and investment houses guarantee payment in the event of damage or financial loss and accept the financial risk for liability that stems from giving the guarantee.

Advantages:

- Pre-approval/proof of funds available online in five minutes.
- High leverage.
- Low fees.
- Founded by investors to improve upon traditional lenders' limitations.

Disadvantages:

- $150 charge for each draw.
- Only available for one- to four-unit properties, not commercial properties.

Partnering Options: Real estate partnership is also called real estate limited partnership (RELP). A partnership is formed by two or more investors who combine their capital and expertise to purchase, develop, or lease property. More so, it can provide a wider pool of knowledge, skills, and contacts, and moral support for an investor.

The major components of any real estate investment are the *seller, the buyer (investor), the property, the source of funds,* and if you are flipping, *the end buyer*. A partnership agreement may require each investor to be actively involved in the partnership as equal members. However, it is common for a real estate partnership to have a general partner who assumes more responsibility and liability for a bigger share of the profits while the other members are limited or passive partners.

Real estate partnerships are categorized into *passive and active partnerships.*

- **Active partnership:** In this structure, all the partners are involved actively in the day-to-day running of the business. For example, one partner could be in charge of financing, while another oversees property management. Such property partnership aims to allow each partner to operate in their areas of strength.
- **Passive partnership:** In this kind of arrangement, one partner does all the work while the other provides the capital. This could mean an investor providing the funds for the investment while a capable team handles the rest. Then the partners agree on how the profits will be shared. This could also be a hands-off approach that investors can use to get funding for their real estate investment.

It is vital to note that partnerships do not always have to be a 50-50 split. Whoever the primary investor (either you or your partner) is and they are doing most of the legwork; they are entitled to a higher percentage of the profits. This is because they are doing all the research to find discounted properties, negotiating the terms of the sale, overseeing the remodeling of the property (if need be), and finding an end buyer. Also, if they are putting down money and/or providing part of the purchase money, under some or all of the above scenarios, they will certainly be entitled to a higher percentage of the profits.

Partnerships in real estate can be set up in:

1. *LLC* (Limited Liability Company): This is the process where a real estate investment becomes a legal entity of its own. This implies that a real estate LLC can have its bank account, tax ID

number, and conduct real estate investing business all under its name. Therefore, with a loss, the property bears the risk/loss not affecting the investor and partners.
2. *LLP* (Limited Liability Partnership): This is a type of partnership in which some or all the partners have limited liabilities. Therefore, it can exhibit features of both a corporation and a partnership. This is suitable for active partnerships, where all the partners want an active role in the investment.
3. *S-Corporation: This is also called the S subchapter. It refers to a corporation that gives the benefits of incorporation while enjoying the tax-exempt benefits of a partnership.*

To have a profitable partnership, you must know what goal you want to achieve and the people you want to partner with. The following tips will help you choose the right partner(s).

1. Decide if going into a partnership is ideal for you, or if you are more comfortable working alone without having to report to or seek other people's opinions.
2. Analyze your strengths and weaknesses and that of each partner to see if they can give you strength in the areas where you are weak and vice versa.
3. Discuss with each partner your business philosophy, investment goals, and the methods used to measure the success of the partnership. Once you have identified potential partners and received a verbal commitment, evaluate the expected success of the partnership.
4. Choose partners who have a similar investment timeline like you to ensure they won't quit before the exit strategy of your real estate partnership can be fully executed.
5. Clearly define roles and expectations by talking to other investors who have formed real estate partnerships or those who are working with your real estate mentor.
6. Construct a written partnership agreement or LLC agreement

with the help of your real estate attorney or financial advisor who has experience in corporate law and finance. This is to restrict a partner from taking out another mortgage or selling the property out from under you and to protect you and your partners from potential liability.
7. Whether you choose an LLC, LLP, or S- Corporation, pick a name that is easy to pronounce as well as memorable for your partnership. Be sure that the name you pick does not infringe on any trademark or copyright law. Finally, if you are stuck on deciding a name for your partnership, some websites can help you generate business names.

Advantages:

- For investors who do not have the funds to invest in real estate, partnerships can help fulfill that dream.
- It enables investors to spread their resources (expertise, time, money) across more deals to increase overall profits.
- It enables investors to fund and complete more complex and expensive deals with higher profit margins.
- Partnerships help to increase an investor's success rate.
- With partnerships, there are shared responsibilities and risks amongst partners.
- Partners can motivate one another to meet their goals.

Disadvantages:

- Benefits of the investment (monthly income, profits from the sale, and tax benefits) are shared amongst partners, thus limiting the potential profits for any one investor.
- Personality conflicts can occur because of different investment and management styles, or when partnership agreements do not clearly define who handles what, where, and when.

- A poorly written partnership agreement can make an excellent investment go bad if responsibilities aren't delegated.
- Capital calls or the need for partners to contribute additional funds can occur if a project isn't playing out to expectations or if one member wants to exit the partnership early and demands to be bought out by the other partners.
- Problems can begin in a real estate partnership if one partner feels they are doing a disproportionate share of the work without getting an equal share of the returns.

Forming a real estate partnership and buying a property with other people is an incredible way to grow your real estate investment portfolio and take your business to the next level. With a partnership, you will raise more investment capital and do better deals while helping others profit from your experience at the same time.

Hard Money Lender Options

9

Getting funds from hard money lenders is an easier alternative investor can use if they are not sure they qualify for loans with traditional lenders like banks or credit unions. This is because hard money loans are given based on the value of the property a person is purchasing and not on their creditworthiness. Specifically, hard money lenders focus on the *after repair value* or ARV, which is an estimate of what the property will be worth once the renovation or development is done.

Hard money loans are sometimes called *bridge loans*. They are short-term asset-based lending options that real estate investors can use to finance an investment project. These short-term loans run between 12 months to five years. Hard money loans are given by private lenders or companies who are often investors too, rather than financial institutions. Sometimes, these loans are offered by individuals who have pooled their money to lend investors for business-related transactions to renovate or developing a property to sell for a profit.

The qualifying criteria for a borrower can vary from lender to lender, but remember that credit scores, payment history, tax returns, and employment status are barely looked into. For this reason, authorizations can happen in days and so can closings. Also, note that if you are new to real estate investing, it is not a bad idea to have a real estate investor credibility kit on hand in case you are asked for it. Normally, it includes a list of properties from your portfolio and a business statement, before-and-after pictures, and escrow closing statements. This summarizes your real estate investing knowledge and successes. Although you may not need it it can improve your chances for approval if you have it.

Hard Money Terms

- Loan-to-value: The loan-to-value (LTV) ratio is the percentage of the property's current value (which is the purchase price at the time the loan was applied for). This percentage loaned is determined by what the lender expects the property will sell for if the investor defaults and the asset needs to be recovered. The LTV ratio is usually between 60 and 70 percent of a property's price but can go as high as 85 percent. In terms of dollars, loan amounts can usually range from $50,000 to five million dollars.
- Points: To make closing costs more efficient, hard money lenders charge a percentage of the loan amount as a one-time fee, instead of detailing the individual costs of processing the loan. This percentage (called points) is between two and 10 percent of the loan amount and is based on the loan-to-value of the property, the complexity of the transaction, and the evaluated risk of the borrower and the asset. Points are normally paid upfront.
- Interest rates: Interest rates for hard money differ from other types of real estate loans. Rates for traditional mortgages can be as low as three-and-a-half to four percent, depending on the

borrower's credit-worthiness and the amount of the property being mortgaged. However, interest rates for hard money range between 10 and 15 percent and can even be as high as 20 percent. The difference is large because of the higher risk of lending hard money and the shorter loan period. It is important to note that usury laws, which vary by state, limit the interest rates that can be charged by lenders and that these rates are a maximum between 10 and 20 percent, which is the typical rate charged for hard money.

- Down payments: Since hard money loans are only given at a percentage of the property's purchase price, down payments are considerably higher than when buying with conventional loans or cash. Instead of a standard 10 percent deposit, or less than five percent as with VA and FHA (203)k loans, in hard money loans, the down payment is the balance not covered by the loan. Therefore, if the loan-to-value of a property is calculated at 60 percent, the deposit will be 40 percent. To close this percentage gap and reduce the added extravagant cost of buying a property, some investors will take out a second hard money loan from a lender who's willing to be in a secondary lien position *(this is a position in which the ranking of the debt in the event of a bankruptcy and liquidation comes after first-lien debt is fully repaid)*.

Advantages:

- Applying for a mortgage is time-consuming, as it can take months to close on a loan, which puts investors at risk of losing out on a particular investment property. With a hard money loan, it is possible to get funding in a matter of weeks.
- Since hard money loans are given by private lenders, investors can have more room for negotiation of the loan terms. You may fix the repayment schedule as is comfortable for you or get certain fees reduced or removed during the underwriting process.

- With a hard money loan, the property itself usually serves as collateral for the loan. Lenders may cut investors some slack by allowing them to secure the loan using personal assets such as a retirement account or a residential property they own.

Disadvantages:

- Hard money loans are easy to get, but investors pay a fee for borrowing this way. The rate of this fee can be up to 10 percentage points higher than a conventional loan. Origination fees, loan-servicing fees, and closing costs are also likely to cost investors more.
- The purpose of a hard money loan is to help an investor get a property ready to go on the market as soon as possible. Because of this, hard money loans have shorter repayment terms than traditional mortgage loans. When choosing a hard money lender, you must have a crystal clear idea of how soon the property will become profitable to ensure that you can repay the loan in time.

When deciding which hard money lender to borrow from, pay close attention to the fees, interest rates, and loan terms. If you end up paying too much for a hard money loan or cut the repayment period too short, that can influence how profitable your real estate venture will be in the long run.

401K, IRA, Whole Life Insurance, and TSP (Thrift Savings Plan)
10

A **401(k) plan** is a tax-advantaged, defined-contribution retirement account offered to employees by many employers. It is named after a section of the U.S. Internal Revenue Code. Workers can make payments to their 401(k) accounts through automatic payroll withholding, and their employers can match some or all of those payments. The investment earnings in a traditional 401(k) plan are not taxed until the employee withdraws that money, which is usually after retirement. However, in a Roth 401(k) plan, withdrawals can be tax free.

There are two types of 401K: *traditional 401K and (designated) Roth 401K*. In a *traditional 401(k)*, employee contributions to their account reduce their income taxes for the year they are made, but their withdrawals are still taxed upon retirement. While with a *designated Roth 401K*, employees make contributions to their account with post-tax income and can still make tax-free withdrawals. 401(k) plans can be a great way for employees to save for retirement. However, it is not as straightforward as other funding options.

As an investor, you cannot invest in real estate directly from a 401K account, but you can choose to roll a former employer's 401k account into an individual retirement account, or IRA. Although many IRA providers don't offer the ability to buy real estate, some offer an account type known as a *self-directed IRA* (which is an IRA that allows you to invest your funds how you want). Please note that the possibility of using an active 401K is not as easy as when you have an old 401K account that you're trying to transfer from a former employer to a new one. In summary, you must no longer have active employment with the company that gave you the 401K account if you want to roll it over.

A self-directed IRA can be traditional or Roth in nature. For example, if you have a Roth 401k, you can roll the funds into a self-directed Roth IRA. While most self-directed IRAs opened to buy real estate are done with large rolled-over accounts, you can also open a self-directed IRA to fund continuously.

To start the rollover process, find an IRA provider that offers real estate services then open the rollover real estate IRA at the new provider. Get the additional account information including account number, address where funds will be sent, and contact information of your account manager after which you should call your 401K plan administrator and request a rollover package. Finish the rollover package paperwork using the new rollover IRA information in the section labeled as a *direct rollover*. Direct rollovers send funds to the new custodian instead of liquidating assets and sending you a check, known as an indirect rollover. Submit the forms and wait four to six weeks for the funds to be transferred. The next step is to find the property you wish to buy and tell your IRA provider to get it. If you don't have enough money in the IRA to buy the property in cash, you will need to open a limited liability company (LLC) that partners with your IRA. The LLC will then get the mortgage and handle Unrelated Business Income Taxes (UBIT) that will come from the non-IRA percentage of income.

It is vital to note that properties gotten through IRS must be for investment only and not personal use. Also, any expenses the property requires must be funded by the IRA and not your money. For this reason, it is necessary to leave some amount of money in your IRA for unforeseen repairs. Personal properties you already own cannot be used on the property, the rental income goes to the IRA and not directly to you. Finally, you cannot buy a property you or a relative already own in a self-directed IRA.

Advantages:

- The income from a rental property funded by the IRA is tax free. Even when the property is sold, it is free from capital gains.
- When a bank sends money to your IRA, it is termed a non-recourse loan. This means in case an investor cannot pay the loan, the bank cannot take any other asset apart from the property which the IRA was gotten for.

Disadvantages:

- Since banks cannot take any other asset apart from the one bought with the IRA (non-recourse loan), the down payment is significantly higher than other options. The down payment is usually 40 percent of the purchase price of the asset.
- Even though IRAs are tax-advantaged accounts, the portion of

your profits that is gotten from a mortgage might be taxable. UBIT (Unrelated Business Income Tax) is a type of tax that might apply to the profits from your real estate investment, so check with a tax professional to see how it could affect you.
- The interest rate on a non-recourse loan is higher by several percentages than the national average for mortgage purchases.

IRA (Individual Retirement Account) is a tax-advantaged account that people used to save and invest for their retirement. The Internal Revenue Service (IRS) also uses individual retirement arrangements (IRAs) to generally mean individual retirement accounts, individual retirement annuities, and other trusts and custodial accounts that act as a personal savings plan with tax advantages for keeping money for retirement.

There are four different IRAs: *traditional IRAs, Roth IRAs, SEP (Simplified Employee Pension) IRAs, and SIMPLE (Savings Incentive Match Plan for Employees) IRAs.* Each of these has different rules regarding eligibility, taxation, and withdrawals. Investments in IRAs can include many financial products, including stocks, bonds, exchange-traded funds (ETFs), and mutual funds.

Individual taxpayers can set up either a traditional IRA or Roth IRA, while small-business owners and self-employed individuals can start SEP and SIMPLE IRAs. An IRA must be opened with an institution that has received Internal Revenue Service (IRS) approval to offer these accounts. Potential options for opening an IRA account include banks, brokerage companies/ brokers, federally insured credit unions, and savings and loan associations. It is common to see many individual investors set up IRAs with brokers. As an investor, your income and your retirement plan will determine which types of IRAs you can open and whether your payments into the account will be tax deductible. Since IRAs are meant for retirement savings, there is an early withdrawal penalty of 10 percent if you withdraw money before age 59½. Depending on the type of IRA you have, you may also need to pay income tax for your early withdrawal.

Traditional and Roth IRAs have been explained under 401K above. But with *SEP IRA,* self-employed persons like independent contractors, freelancers, and small-business owners can set up SEP IRAs. A SEP IRA follows the same taxation rules for withdrawals as a traditional IRA. Business owners who set up SEP IRAs for their employees can deduct the payments they make for the employees. However, the employees may not contribute to their accounts, and the IRS taxes their withdrawals as though it is income. The *SIMPLE IRA* is also for small businesses and self-employed individuals, and it obeys the same tax rules for withdrawals as a traditional IRA. However, unlike SEP IRAs, SIMPLE IRAs allow employees to make payments to their accounts, and the employer must make payments as well. All the payments are tax deductible thus, possibly helping the business or employee move into a lower tax bracket.

Whole Life Insurance is the original life insurance policy that provides insurance permanently unlike termed life insurance, which runs for some years. It provides coverage for the life of the insured person and pays a death benefit. Whole life insurance also has a savings component in which cash value can accumulate. Growing cash value is an essential component of whole life insurance and in the savings, component interest may grow on a tax-deferred basis. To grow your cash value, you can send in payments more than the scheduled premium. Dividends can be reinvested into the cash value and earn interest.

This cash value provides a living benefit to the policyholder. This means that the cash value serves as a source of equity. To access cash reserves, the policyholder (you) requests a withdrawal of funds or a loan, and interest is charged on loans with varying rates for each policyholder. It is also vital to remember unpaid loans reduce the death benefit by the amount owed and that withdrawals reduce the cash value but not the death benefit.

The advantage a policyholder has is that they can withdraw tax-free funds up to the value of total premiums paid. This is why policyholders should send payments that are more than the scheduled premium.

With the opportunity of taking a loan from the cash reserve of a whole life insurance policy, investors can make a withdrawal or take loans to invest in real estate.

Advantages:

- Helps you build cash value you can borrow from or withdraw before death.
- It has fixed premiums.
- There is a guarantee of returns on premium paid even though it is modest.

Disadvantages:

- People with unstable cash flow cannot have a whole life insurance policy as they will face difficulties with paying the premium.
- Premiums are expensive.
- The cash value of a whole life insurance policy yields profitable returns when it has been held for a minimum of 20 years.
- Can be complicated to understand, especially as the return on the policy is not spelled out on the policy but would need to be calculated.

TSP (Thrift Savings Plan)[11] is one of three retirement benefits federal employees and members of the uniformed services are privileged to have. This 401(k)-style benefit lets you save for retirement, but with the option to take a loan from your contributions for general use or to buy your primary residence. Borrowing from your TSP contributions is a simple way to get the down payment and closing costs for your first residential property. However, the loan is limited to the funds you have contributed to your TSP account (not including the matching funds from your agency or service and any accrued earnings).

TSP loans must be between $1,000 and $50,000. However, only employee (borrower's) contributions, not government contribution portions, are used to fund the loans. Also, a $50 processing fee gets added to your loan as well.

Advantages:

- Interest from a TSP loan gets paid to the borrower's TSP account, not a commercial lender. In a nutshell, the borrower pays themselves interest.
- Applying for a TSP loan is easy, and there are no denials as long as there's enough money in a borrower's account.
- If a borrower defaults on their TSP loan, their credit isn't affected because even though the remaining balance becomes taxable income, the default isn't reported to credit bureaus.
- A borrower can pay off the loan in installments as needed. This could involve changing repayment details such as extending the payback time for up to 15 years, adjusting the number of payments or their amount.

Disadvantages:

- The loan must be repaid before federal employees retire from service.
- By taking out a TSP loan, a borrower sacrifices their long-term account growth for short-term gain.
- When a TSP account holder pays into a TSP plan, it means they are using pre-tax income. So when they take out a TSP loan, they are using tax-deferred money that is later repaid using taxable income.
- Once a borrower retires and withdraws from their TSP funds they borrowed in the past and repaid using taxable income,

the funds being withdrawn are taxed again. Hence leading to double taxation.

Choosing any of the funding options above to start your real estate investment should be determined by which one is the most beneficial to you. With all their advantages and disadvantages listed out, this should be a walk in the park.

Chapter Summary

In summary:

- Rental property is a home or property bought by an investor who then puts it up for lease to tenants or other types of rental agreements and makes revenue from it.
- Funding is the act of providing the resources to finance a need or project. It could be provided by the government, an organization or group of people, or an individual.
- There are many advantages to investing in real estate, including the fact that the monthly revenue gotten from a rental property increases when there is inflation. Also, unlike the stock market, real estate investment is not volatile. However, to get started with investing in real estate, you need some money. Whether this money is yours, it doesn't matter. What's important is that you have some money to invest in getting your first rental property.

In the next chapter, you will learn how to find the right property.

3

FIND THE RIGHT PROPERTY

Now that you must have picked a funding option, the next step is to find the right property. Buying an investment property is a smart financial decision if done the right way. An investor can get a strong return through passive income, tax breaks, and equity gains[1]. However, getting a massive return on your investment is not a guarantee, therefore, you need to think strategically when choosing and purchasing your investment property. An investor (newbie or veteran) needs to work in line with both market trends and the other factors that dictate whether a real estate investment will succeed.

If you are a newbie in the real estate investment business, it is normal to be overwhelmed by finding the right investment property, as there are many factors to consider when making that final buying decision. Whether you plan to buy a vacation rental property, a condo in the city to rent out year-round, a commercial investment property, or any other type of real estate investment, you must go into it with a clear head and a good understanding of what makes a worthy buy.

The first step I will recommend is that you start a search on your own. It is not a bad idea to seek the help of a professional like a property manager because there are many benefits to it (which will be discussed in the next chapter). However, starting a solo search will eliminate any pressure a property manager might put on you so you can buy.

After starting a search on your own and narrowing down what you want in your investment property, knowing if a property is the right one for you to invest in depends on the following factors:

1. **Location:** Where a property is located will determine whether it will be a successful investment. It will also determine the tenants you get and the vacancy rate. For instance, buying a residential property in an industrialized area is a super wrong investment because nobody wants to live in a noisy environment. Or imagine having students as your tenants, which means every summer you will struggle to make money from rent since they will be on summer vacation. Finally, if you are going to hire a property management company to look after your property, the proximity of the property to where you live is less of an issue. If you intend to actively manage your investment property yourself, get a property that is close to where you live.
2. **The difference in the down payment:** When you are buying an investment property, the down payment is not the same as when you are buying a standard family home. For a standard family home, the down payment can be as low as 1 to 10 percent while for an investment property, the down payment is *at least* 15 to 20 percent. Investment properties do not qualify for mortgage insurance. Also, there are stricter approval requirements regarding getting funds which leads to the need for a more substantial down payment. Factors that determine how much down payment will be made include an investor's credit score, income, and debt-to-income (DTI) ratio. The smart thing to do when buying real estate is to finish the details regarding funding before going on a property hunt so that you know what's workable and what isn't.
3. **The expected return on the property:** In predicting the

expected returns on your real estate investment, I will recommend you use the 1 percent rule. This 1 percent is what real estate investors used to determine whether a property is worth buying. This rule states that every month you should be able to get an income not less than 1 percent of the price you paid for the property. This includes the purchase price and any additional money spent, such as repairs or renovations. Say, for instance, you buy an investment property for $50,000 and put in $15,000 for renovations, which gives a total initial investment of $65,000. Following this rule, be able to get 1 percent of $65,000 which is a monthly income of $650. Anything short of this might mean the property will not be lucrative. As with all rules, there are some exceptions. If for instance you want to buy a million-dollar property or buy a property in an up-and-coming neighborhood that won't likely see strong returns right away, you might choose to ignore the 1 percent rule and focus long-term instead. To know what your annual return on a property might be and whether it is worth buying it, use an investment property calculator. It will tell you what you will make on the property after calculating the purchase price and expenses.

4. **Expenses to be done on the property:** As much as we would like it to be one, an investment property is not something you buy and decide that you will not spend extra money on. There are mandatory expenses required to maintain any property, and these expenses are both fixed and variable. Also, it is hard to predict either of these expenses with complete accuracy, so you will need a budget for these to make sure you don't end up broke every year. Since variable expenses are more difficult to predict than fixed expenses, just make sure you have enough room in your budget for unexpected repair costs, such as plumbing or roof repair. Fixed expenses you will need to include in your budget:

- Property taxes.
- Homeowner's insurance.
- Property management expenses (where applicable).
- HOA fees (if applicable).
- General upkeep costs (cleaning, landscaping, etc).

Potential risks associated with owning the property

Buying an investment property has its risks, and it is crucial you know what they are. Some of the most prominent risks to keep in mind are:

- Unanticipated rental interest.
- Unforeseen expensive repairs.
- Inflated property taxes.
- Change local market economy.
- Bad tenants that lead to repair costs or even eviction costs.

An investment property can be one of the most profitable purchases that you ever make, so don't allow the risks involved to scare you. But even as you take the risk to invest in real estate, be aware of them so you don't get caught unprepared. You can work with an experienced advisor who can help you navigate the process and make the best purchase possible. They will also help you thoroughly evaluate all the risks above to ensure that the investment you make is smart.

1. Management of the property: Some real estate investors prefer to be hands on with their renters by acting as landlords or managers of the property, and even seeing to the day-to-day operations personally. While others pay a management company to do the work for them because they live far away, do not have the time, or just don't want to be involved that way. Note that even though hiring a property management service is quite an expense, it is not necessarily more expensive than when you decide to do the work on your own. Hiring a property manager might even be cheaper. Do some research to

figure out which would be the better option for you, and then consider these expenses when you decide about buying a property or not.

2. Future development: Find out what plans are in the works for an area by asking the municipal planning department so you can predict what its future will look like. Also, government and council websites often have information on infrastructure project proposals online. Monitor any residential properties that could be developed up near amenities, like schools and shopping hubs.

3. Buy investment properties that appeal to the dominant market in that location: When looking for an investment property to buy, buy one that appeals to the people who are actively renting in that location. For example, a compact unit may be more affordable than a house, but if the local market is dominated by families, your investment property won't entice them. Your rental property will have an advantage if it has features that are useful for your target market e.g. proximity to public transport. Get advice from experienced investors and other experts in the industry about the features your target market is interested in. However, be careful not to trust your investment decisions to someone with a vested interest in selling you something. If the person telling you a location will *boom* will benefit financially when you buy a property there, seek a second opinion, just to be sure.

4. Property taxes: Property taxes will probably differ broadly across your target area, and know how much you will lose in taxes. High property taxes are not always a bad thing. For instance, a good neighborhood that attracts long-term tenants will be beneficial to an investor than an unappealing location that also has high taxes. To find the tax information on the properties in a location, the municipality's assessment office will have all the tax information on file[2]. Conversely, you can talk to homeowners in the community for this information. Also, make sure you find out if property tax increases will

happen soon. Note that a town in financial distress may hike taxes far beyond what a landlord can realistically charge in rent[3].

5. The strategy behind the purchase: As with other things in life, your investment in real estate should have a clear goal. This goal could be to generate income for early retirement or to have money to fund an enormous expense. Whatever the case may be, you need a clear strategy on how you will meet your goals using real estate. If you don't have a strategy, your real estate investment might end up a big fail.

There are many strategies like *buying and selling* (an investor buys a profitable property, fixes it up if need be, and then sell for profit), *buy and hold* (an investor buys a profitable property and holds on to it knowing the value of the property will increase with time), *house flipping* (an investor finds a property that needs fixing, does the renovation and sells for a profit), *live-in-and-rent* (this happens when an investor has a duplex or can afford to rent out a part of his property), etc. Whichever strategy you choose can be accurately defined when you are clear on your goals (short or long term), timeframe (5 – 10 years or more), and risk profile (high or low). You should also consider how involved you want to be based on your available time for research, for looking for property, or for renovating.

With all this firsthand information, as an investor, be able to know the time it will take to double the amount you have invested at a given compound rate. This is determined using a rule called *the Rule of 72*.

This Rule of 72 is a formula used to calculate the time it will take for invested money to double at a compound interest rate. It is calculated as 72 divided by the interest rate. This rule states that compounding interests will double the price of a commodity in the number of years of 72 divided by the yearly interest rate. For example, if you have invested **$20,000, and** it earns **9 percent** per year, to find out how long it will take the $20,000 to double into $40,000, you would divide **72 by 9 percent** which answers to be **8 years**.

If you were to invest for a long time, let's say for 32 years, your $20,000 investment would turn into $40,000 in 8 years, $80,000 in 16 years, $80,000 in 32 years. The Rule of 72 can also leverage (which is using borrowed money to buy a property) to show how you can achieve amazing returns using investment property. Doubling your money every 10 years will not fast-track you to wealth. To get on the fast track to wealth, you must incorporate leverage. With leverage, you control an enormous amount of wealth, while only having invested a small amount of money.

Say, for instance you put down a 20 percent deposit on a $200,000 property, this means you have invested $40,000. Now, if the price of that property doubles to $80,000 in the next 10 years, the Rule of 72 shows that the value of your property will increase at a yearly growth rate of 7.2 percent. The price of the property will be worth $400,000 after the 10-year period. By taking this extra equity and applying it to new property investments, an investor can use the Rule of 72 and leverage many times to become wealthy. This is a proven strategy that has worked countless times and not a theory.

As I stated earlier, going into real estate investing can be daunting, and if you don't have the right guidance, mistakes are inevitable. Many real estate investment experts you see today have made their fair share of mistakes. Even I have made some mistakes in the past. I have also witnessed other real estate investors in my network make mistakes, and I will tell you about them so that you can have a better chance at not making the same mistakes.

Common Mistakes Real Estate Investors Make

Not doing background checks on tenants: I prefer to buy properties that are already rented to reliable tenants. The reason is that it is easier to take over an existing lease than it is to find and approve new tenants. I made this mistake with a house I bought and the outcome was far from pleasant. I had purchased a townhome, which was a fixer-upper. Since I didn't have a property manager my friends and family helped with the remodeling before I put it on the market. When tenants came, I didn't do background checks on them and this was the beginning of my problems. They stopped paying their rents, destroyed my property, and law enforcement had to be involved many times. It got so bad that the families of the tenants sent threats to my family. It was overwhelming, so what I did to salvage the situation was to take out a HELOC on the property to repair all the damages they had caused. Once the property was back in shape, I turned it into a fix and flip, sold it for $90,000, and made $50,000 in profit.

Lessons learned from this experience, here are my three unbreakable rules concerning tenants:

- To always run background checks on tenants before allowing them on my property.
- To hire a property manager and let them take care of anything that concerns the tenants so I do not put my family in harm's way.
- Have tenants sign agreements that stop them from delaying rents and holds them responsible for any damages they cause on the property.

1. **Giving themselves very little time to close:** I know someone in my network who wanted to buy another property, and his lender said he would need at least 30 days to finish the mortgage process. The lender suggested this investor should give himself some time like a 45-day escrow *(this is the use of a third party, which holds an asset or funds before they are transferred from one party to another)* period. But he didn't take his lender's advice. He did not give himself any extra time instead he set the closing date as 30 days from the date he made the offer. By the time they finished the negotiation process and signed the paperwork, they only had 24 days left. Although they finished the underwriting process on-time, when it came down to the wire, it could have fallen through easily. After seeing this experience with my friend, I now insist on a longer close than is necessary when I'm financing an investment property even if it might be a disadvantage for me compared to cash buyers.
2. **I didn't have enough money kept aside for reserves:** lenders for investment properties want to see at least six months'

worth of expenses in reserves. This includes principal, interest, taxes, insurance, and any HOA dues. Say for instance your total monthly payment is $1,000 you will need to have $6,000 in the bank besides your down payment and closing costs. I didn't plan for this when I bought my first property so consequently; I ended up keeping more cash than I had expected aside. The bottom line is, having a down payment is not enough to get an investment property mortgage. The requirements are usually different for each lender, so ask what you will want to see before you make offers.

3. **I was not ready for repair costs:** Remember the story I told you about how tenants stopped paying rent and did lots of damages on my townhouse property, let's just say the repairs I had to do on the property were not something I'd planned for. What made it worse was, I did not have any insurance, specifically landlord insurance, to help with the repairs on the property so I had to fund it from the HELOC I took.

For me the lessons are:

- To have landlord insurance on my property for situations like this. Having insurance helps take away the burden of repair costs.
- I will make a budget for the unforeseen repairs that may need to be done within the next year or two. I won't just budget for the repairs the property needs at the moment.
- **I did not know peak rental season:** My rental property is in a trendy neighborhood approximately one mile from a university campus. For this reason, properties in this area appeal to college students more than any other demographic. Even with this advantage, I didn't know college students like to sort out their housing for the upcoming school year in June and July but some extend to August. Since I had closed on the property in mid-July, the extensive renovations were not done until the third week of August. By then, the university was back

in session and almost all college students had found where to live. We had to come up with creative strategies to get the units occupied with tenants. Now I know that if the property had been on the market a few weeks earlier, we wouldn't have had to reduce the rent just to get tenants. Also, if I had known the peak rental season, it would have helped with planning the renovation and getting the property on the market early.

Conclusively, when finding the right rental property, it should be one with good cash flow and the ability to produce high ROI whether the market is up or down. It is important to know that inflation also helps a landlord earn more because then the prices of rent also increase.

Now that you know what to look out for when finding the right property, and you have glimpsed how a property manager can be a huge help in finding the right property, you have the option to hire one or use software that can help you manage your property. If using property management software feels like a better option for you, I will suggest you try using *Buildium* to see if it is your cup of tea. If it doesn't suit your needs, there is other software available for you to choose from.

However, if hiring a property manager seems like the best choice for you, in the next chapter I will show you how to find a property manager.

Chapter Summary

In summary:

- The first step I will recommend in finding the right property is that you start a search on your own. It is not a bad idea to seek the help of a professional like a property manager because there are many benefits to it (which will be discussed in the next chapter). However, starting a solo search will eliminate any pressure a property manager might put on you so you can buy.

- The Rule of 72 is a formula that is used to calculate the time it will take for invested money to double at a compound interest rate. It is calculated as 72, divided by the interest rate. This rule states that compounding interests will double the price of a commodity in the number of years of 72 divided by the yearly interest rate.
- When finding the right rental property, it should be one with good cash flow and the ability to produce high ROI whether the market is up or down.

In the next chapter, you will learn how to find a property manager.

4

FIND A PROPERTY MANAGER

A property manager is a person or firm given the responsibility to operate a real estate property for a fee. The reason an investor would hire a property manager could be because they cannot attend to such details for whatever reason (lack of time, distance, inexperience, etc) or is not even interested in doing so.

Owning a rental property is a rewarding experience because it generates a steady flow of passive income. However, a rental property can only make money for its owner when there are good tenants who pay their rent on time and do not destroy the property. But once a landlord gets a difficult tenant, having and managing a rental property becomes hard and time-consuming. This is when using a professional property management company becomes helpful for the landlords, especially when they own multiple properties.

How to Find a Property Manager

[1]All property managers do not work the same way. Some specialize in single-family rentals while others specialize in small multifamily properties. In larger metro areas, some property managers only work in

specific locations or with certain property classes such as brand new Class A homes, Class B workforce housing, or Class C cash cow rental property. Here's how to find a good property manager for your real estate business.

1. **Ask for referrals:** Good sources where you can ask for property manager referrals are *fellow real estate investors, real estate agents, and brokers, real estate attorneys, mortgage brokers, escrow companies, contractors, e.g. HVAC and landscaping companies.*
2. **Look up property management companies online:** If you are just investing in real estate and doing it long distance, you may still build your local real estate team. Fortunately, there are many ways to research property managers online if you are looking to add one to your team:

- Search the internet for *residential property manager + your city name.*
- Use Yelp and Better Business Bureau for ratings, customer, and client reviews.
- Craigslist ads are good for finding the adverts of property managers.
- Roofstock helps you find vetted property managers with ongoing performance monitoring.

Conduct a standard interview:

It is important to interview many property managers as part of your initial interview process just to know the right fit for your needs. Some important questions to ask when interviewing a real estate property manager should include:

- Number of years in business.
- Staff strength, including full-time and part-time workers.

- Number of properties under their management the current and previous year.
- Average time current clients have been with the property management company.
- Areas in the city where the properties are located.
- Average percentage of vacant properties.
- How the property manager determines fair market rents.
- Their process for finding and vetting tenants for approval.
- The frequency of property management inspections and owner reports.
- How and when owner distributions are made.
- If they have online systems like owner portal, tenant rent payments, and repair requests.
- Other services are offered like leasing and brokerage, and if the property managers have a dedicated staff for these extra tasks.
- If there is an availability of in-house repair people.
- Is there any sort of education, training, and licensing of property management staff?
- Ask for the background of the property management company owners.
- Do they have awards and other recognition within the local community?

Verify their certifications and licenses

Property managers in most states are expected to have both a real estate license and a general business license. You can verify that the licenses are active and in good standing by checking with the Department of Real Estate and Secretary of State offices.

Other common credentials a property manager may have are:

- IREM – Institute of Real Estate Management.
- CAI – Community Association Institute.
- NAA – National Apartment Association.

- NARPM – National Association of Residential Property Managers.

Understand your property management contract

A property management agreement is a legally contract between a landlord and the property management company. The terms and conditions of a property management agreement are based on state laws and regulations from the department of real estate.

When reviewing a property management contract, these are the key areas to look out for:

- The start and end date of the property management agreement.
- Compensation structure such as fixed fee versus percentage of revenue, leasing fees, and new account start-up fees.
- Charges for extra services such as overseeing major remodeling and tenant evictions.
- The frequency of financial reporting and communication.
- Timing of owner disbursements after rent has been collected, and the operating expenses paid.
- The landlord's responsibilities include maintaining a reserve account and getting sufficient insurance coverage.
- Things the landlord is restricted from doing like finding tenants, entering the property without notice, and listing the property for sale without informing the property manager.
- Agreement to abide by local, state, and federal fair housing laws.
- Insurance carried by property managers should include errors and omissions coverage and general liability insurance.
- Property manager liability *holds harmless* clauses and a *reasonable care* clause that shows the manager will take reasonable care when hiring third-party contractors.
- Automatic renewal clause and how much notice must be given.

- Early termination clause that includes how much notice must be given, the fee for ending the contract early, and obligations upon termination e.g. providing copies of all tenant leases and sending funds to the landlord.

Ask for work references

The last step in choosing a property manager for your rental property is to ask for references and samples of their work. This is just to make sure the only ratings they have are real. To get the work samples you can do:

- Talk to current clients of the property manager who own similar properties to yours to see how satisfied they are with the property manager's services and if there are any areas, the manager could improve in.
- Have one of your team members drive by several properties the company manages. They should look out for red flags such as many "For rent" signs and obvious signs of damages.

Factors to Consider When Choosing a Property Manager

If a landlord makes the mistake of hiring the wrong property manager for their specific type of investment property, it can lead to decreased cash flow due because of the high vacancy rate. For this same reason, put in the extra time and effort to find a great property manager that will screen potential tenants so that your cash flow isn't affected.

Listed are important factors to consider when looking for a rental property manager.

1. What will the communication be like? Will it be by phone, email, or text?
2. What will be the frequency of communication?
3. How quickly and professionally will the property manager respond to inquiries or complaints?
4. Do they have experience with my specific type of rental property investment?
5. What is their historical track record of filling vacancies at the fair market rent?
6. What knowledge of basic accounting practices for income, tax, and real estate investment purposes do they have?
7. Do they use any technology or software to organize and automate the property management process?
8. How does the property manager's fee structure compare to other companies in the same market?

Duties of a Property Manager

Knowing what the duties of a property manager are will help you know if they are doing their jobs efficiently. Property management fees are usually between 8 and 12 percent of the gross rent collected. This certainly takes a huge chunk of your cash flow, so you need to make sure you are getting your money's worth in their services.

1. Property maintenance and repairs that keep the property in good operating condition.
2. Property inspections including tenant move-in walk-throughs and move-out inspections, routine interior and exterior inspections, and drive-by inspections.
3. Market vacant space for rent.
4. Tenant screening and lease signing.
5. Setting fair market rent and collecting the rent.
6. Collect rent when due and make timely disbursements to the landlord.
7. Create an operating budget in agreement with the landlord and manage the budget.
8. Schedule and track the progress of maintenance requests.
9. Handle tenant issues promptly when they arise.
10. Manage finances and record-keeping, including payment of vendor invoices and providing monthly and annual operating statements to the landlord.

Importance/ Benefits of Hiring a Property Manager

[2]Although many investors still prefer to use the DIY approach to manage their investment properties. Many investors have learned to embrace hiring a property manager to help them run their real estate investment success. Below are the advantages of hiring a property manager.

1. **It gives you more time to do other things:** Many things will demand your time. For example, putting up rental ads, replying to messages, meeting prospective tenants, and dealing with maintenance or repair issues. The time doing all these will take is certainly multiplied by the number of rental properties you have. Therefore, hiring a property manager takes away these responsibilities from your schedule to give you time to do other things like work at your job or expand

your business. If real estate investment is a full-time job for you, hiring a property manager will give you enough time to scout for more properties and expand your portfolio.
2. **You can avoid having legal problems:** Experienced landlords know that one bad tenant can cause a great deal of financial and legal headaches. A high-quality property management company has a vast knowledge of local regulations and laws, and they can protect you from potential lawsuits and vulnerabilities. Because each state has its laws that can affect a landlord, there are also federal laws that will cover the following areas:

- Screening tenants.
- The condition of the property and its safety.
- Tenant evictions.
- Unit inspections.
- Signing and ending leases.
- Collecting and handling rent and security deposits.

If you can avoid one lawsuit by hiring a property manager, it will be cheaper than having to pay the tenant who sued you for compensation. More so, you will avoid wasting your time and energy during the process of the lawsuit. Last, it is the job of a property manager to make sure you comply with all the landlord-tenant laws.

1. **You can avoid dealing with the clients directly:** Some landlords enjoy building relationships with their tenants, but many prefer not to have to deal with them at all, especially when things don't go well. A property manager sees two' tenants' complaints so that you don't have to worry about sorting out those issues. As the landlord, there is a tendency to take things personally when you have to respond to a difficult tenant. But a property manager handles disagreements objectively and professionally.
2. **Their experience comes in handy for different situations:**

Depending on how long they have been in the business, a property manager has years of experience managing homes therefore, they have a defined work process. Some companies go as far as posting each step of their work process on their website. Many property managers are also licensed real estate agents so they know the ins and outs of the market, how to price homes (renting or selling) etc. In the course of their work, they have had to settle disputes with tenant, roommate changes, lease breaks, evictions, etc. All of which can overwhelm a newbie landlord.

3. **Property managers help you have short vacancy periods and help with long tenant retention:** A common misconception people have is thinking that once a tenant signs a lease for your property, then the storm is over. But one thing you have to remember as a landlord is that your tenant will not live in your property forever because they will have to move someday, and for whatever reason. Long vacancy periods decrease profits and stop cash flow therefore you need to get a new, qualified tenant into your property as soon as possible once the current tenant leaves. Property managers are used to tenants leaving at a moment's notice, and so they are prepared to market the home and getting it ready for rent once again. A good property manager has a tenant retention policy that is time-tested. They are also good at retaining tenants by making them satisfied with their live-in condition, so they feel like they are in good hands. A happy tenant will probably rent long-term than one who is not happy with the property or with the landlord.

A good property manager will handle the following tasks to prevent your properties from staying vacant for too long:

- **Prepare the properties for rent:** A property manager will know the fixes that must be done to the property to maximize your revenue.
- **Determine the optimal rent rate:** Setting the rent too high

might cause long vacancy periods, but charging too low will cause the loss of money every month. Therefore, it is important to set the right price for your property, and doing it requires knowledge of the local real estate market, data on similar units, and access to professional rental rate tools.
- **Marketing your property effectively:** Skilled property managers are skilled at writing ads and, so they know what to say and where to advertise to get many candidates quickly. They are familiar with sales and know how to close deals when they get field calls from prospects.

1. **Collection of rent is more efficient:** As I stated earlier, property managers can handle situations with tenants effectively and professionally. The same applies to collecting rent from tenants. The property manager lets the tenants know the payment clause on the lease contract and how important it is not to breach the contract. To ensure consistent and reliable cash flow, rent must be collected on time every month. As expected, there will be months your tenants will come up with one reason or the other why they cannot meet up with paying the rent that month. Of course, you are human and there is a tendency for you to feel empathetic and give them more time, even when it is not favorable for you. This kind gesture may be taken for granted by a tenant who may see you as too permissive. By hiring a property manager, you will not have to deal with the excuses tenants will bring, nor will you have to deal with evicting a tenant if it comes to that.
2. **Low cost of repair and maintenance:** When you hire a property manager you gain access to professional maintenance and a network of licensed, insured, and bonded contractors. The property manager will use contractors who are trustworthy and are known for delivering quality work with good pricing. This will save you a lot of money compared to hiring someone you don't know by yourself. A property

manager can get discounts for maintenance and repairs services because they have many properties they manage.
3. **A good property manager will help you increase the value of your property:** An excellent property manager knows that preventive maintenance is the best way to keep a property's value high and even possibly increase it. This requires regular maintenance checks and inspections, a written maintenance schedule, and detailed documentation. An agency may also offer you valuable feedback and suggestions on upgrades and modifications that the tenants prefer. An excellent property manager knows that preventive maintenance is the best way to keep a property's value high and even possibly increase it.
4. **Less stress and more freedom:** The advantage of hiring a property manager is that you don't have to attend to late-night emergencies, eviction process, going after tenants for their rent, fix damages, paperwork, and look for contractors, or do other difficult and time-consuming duties. With a property manager doing all this for you, you can travel anywhere you want without worrying about your tenants or the routine inspections. You can even live far away from your property and have the freedom to invest in other properties.

Disadvantages of Hiring a Property Manager

As with everything, hiring a property manager has its disadvantages, and some of those are:

1. **Hiring a property manager will cost more money:** A property manager takes a cut from your rental income. They charge between 5 to 10 percent of the rent for each unit or property they manage for you. This charge is besides any other fees due to them. Some ask for a placement fee, which is up to one month's rent when they bring in a new tenant. Sometimes, additional costs for maintenance work may be demanded. So you must calculate all these potential costs and know how

much from your rental income you can spare, then negotiate their payment before you hire a property manager. Also, note that some companies have a low management fee but then subtly charge extra fees where other companies might not. So before sure to compare costs and payment plans before you hire a property manager.
2. **Some Property Managers May be Dishonest:** The reason you employed a manager property is that you trust they work hard to bring in tenants and manage your money honestly. Unfortunately, all property managers are not honest or competent. They even have the chance to collect extra money from tenants and keep it for themselves or overcharge you for maintenance work. Managing your properties is the only way to prevent anyone from taking advantage of you. However, if you plan to hire a property manager or a property management company, check with those they have worked with before to see if they are honest and competent.
3. **No involvement in the management process by the landlord:** If you prefer a hands-on approach to do things, hiring a property manager will not satisfy your need for wanting to be in charge. This is because property managers operate on their own. After all, they are experienced in doing so. They only get the landlord involved when the situation demands it. So if you want to be involved in managing your property, I will advise you not to hire a property manager because it will only leave you dissatisfied.

Although hiring a property manager is an expense, the advantages outweigh the disadvantages for many investors. If you can afford to hire a property manager, your life will be less stressful and you will have the time to focus on other ventures. Weigh your options and honestly ask yourself if you can hand over the affairs of your property to another person and if you can't, find out if you will be committed to managing your property effectively. This will help you decide whether you will need a property manager.

Chapter Summary

In summary:

- A property manager is a person or firm given the responsibility to operate a real estate property for a fee. The reason an investor would hire a property manager could be because they cannot attend to such details for whatever reason (lack of time, distance, inexperience, etc) or are not even interested in doing so.
- Knowing what the duties of a property manager are will help you know if they are doing their jobs efficiently. Property management fees are usually between 8 and 12 percent of the gross rent collected.
- If a landlord makes the mistake of hiring the wrong property manager for their specific type of investment property, it can lead to decreased cash flow due because of the high vacancy rate. For this same reason, put in the extra time and effort to find a great property manager that will screen potential tenants so that your cash flow isn't affected.

In the next chapter, you will learn how to close on a property.

5

CLOSE ON THE PROPERTY

A real estate deal is a long and tedious process that involves many procedures, paperwork, and formalities. **Closing** is the process of signing the papers that make a property yours. But before the closing happens, there are a lot of things that need to be done. Whether you are buying your first property or buying a new property after selling the old one, you cannot move into your property or put it for rent until you officially close on the property (sign the papers).

The closing day, which is the day you meet with the seller, your real estate agents, title or escrow agents, and other people involved in the transaction, is the day the property officially becomes yours. Because of the complexity of a real estate closing process, you might consider hiring an attorney to help you out.

However, the closing process[1] starts immediately after the seller accepts your purchase offer, which is usually 30 to 60 days before the actual closing date. This timeframe should hold if all things work according to plan, such as no loan underwriting problem or no major defect is found out during a routine home inspection.

During this closing period, the sale of the property is said to be pending. If you can make an ample deposit of up to 10 percent of the agreed purchase price into an escrow account once your offer is accepted, you can refer to the closing process as the *escrow period*. This means the home you are buying is in escrow until the closing day.

PS: An escrow account is an account held by a third party on behalf of the buyer and seller. It is where the deposit and other documents are kept until everything about the transaction is done. Once the closing is completed, the deposit and documents are then given to the seller and buyer, respectively.

Except you are buying a property with cash, get pre-approved for a mortgage before you even start looking for a property. Though being pre-approved is not a yardstick for closing a deal, most sellers just naturally expect property buyers to have a mortgage pre-approval letter. This is because having one can make the closing process quicker and even give you more bargaining power during negotiation. What this shows the seller is that you have strong financial backing.

Having a pre-approved mortgage further helps you know to save time and effort and allows you to look for only properties that are within your budget. Mortgage pre-approval also gives you more time to respond to rejection. It can help you stop a lender from making you miss out on a good deal and delaying your dreams if they disapprove of you.

Below is a breakdown of the general series of events that happen during the residential real estate closing process, which happens after the seller has accepted your offer. I will show you what you need to provide and how much you are expected to disburse before and on the closing day. I will also cover the documents and disclosures you should understand and sign to make the transaction official. This is to show you that no matter how complex closing might seem, with these steps[2] written out for you, closing on a property will be a walk in the park.

1. **Title search and insurance:** After getting an escrow account, which I consider the first step, the next thing to do is to get a title search and insurance check. The essence of doing this so

you can have legal protection in the sense of when you buy a property, no other person can claim it in the future or so you can avoid being scammed into buying a property that someone else has already paid for. A *title search* is the act of searching public records to confirm the legal ownership of a property and to find out if there are any claims on the property. And if there are, they should be resolved before the buyer gets the property. *Title insurance* protects the real estate owner and lenders from financial loss gotten from problems relating to title defects in a property.
2. **Get an attorney:** Although hiring a legal expert is compulsory, it is smart to get a professional legal opinion on your closing documents, especially with the complicated terms that can be difficult to understand, even for well-educated individuals. For a reasonable fee, getting the opinion of an experienced real estate attorney can be beneficial, such as giving hints for any potential problems in the paperwork.
3. **Home and pest inspection:** Once the seller accepts your purchase offer, schedule a home inspection so you see exactly what you are paying for. The reason for this inspection is to look for both minor and major fixes on the property, such as structural problems, faulty appliances, elements that may violate local building codes, and pest infestation. If you inspect a property and find a tremendous problem with the property during the inspection, you can decide to let the purchase fall through or ask the seller to do the repairs before you buy. Alternatively, you can tell the seller to pay you to fix the repairs if your purchase offer included a home inspection contingency. A pest inspection differs from a home inspection and it is carried out by an expert to ensure the property does not have any destructive insects. Pests that can destroy woods should be taken care of at a reasonable fee before the property is paid for. And just like repairs, you can tell the owner to have it fixed or ask that they pay you to fix it. Finally, even if pest inspections are not

compulsory in your state, it is better you still do it to be on the safe side.

4. **Renegotiate your offer on the property:** If after inspecting a property and you find damages, renegotiate your offer on the property even if your offer has been accepted before. Your renegotiation should reflect the cost of fixing any damages that will cost you or you can leave the offer the same way, provided the seller will take care of the repairs. If the seller refuses to do so, you can back out on the deal.

5. **Get lender appraisal:** It is normal for lenders to protect their investments or try to minimize the losses by commissioning an appraisal during the underwriting process *(the process whereby a lender reviews a loan application to determine the amount of risk involved)*. Normally buyers pay the appraisal fee by the appraisal date, or on the closing date. This appraisal fee is almost the same amount as the home inspection fee. If your appraiser sees that the property is worth much as you have agreed to pay for it, then all is good. But if the appraisal portrays the value of the property as less than the accepted purchase price, the lender will lend the amount of the property's appraised value. A low appraisal would require the buyer and seller of the property to renegotiate the purchase price as well as amend the purchase agreement which can delay the closing.

6. **Lock in your interest rate:** Interest rates can change and depend on many factors, such as geographic region, property type, type of loan applied for, and the applicant's credit score. For this reason, I will advise you to lock in the interest rate for the loan you want to get in advance. This will save you from being tossed about by market fluctuations, which causes interest rates to increase before you can even close on your property purchase. No matter how little the increase in the interest rate is, it can increase your monthly payments and the time to repay the mortgage.

7. **Take away any contingency:** Your real estate offer should depend on the following:

- Collecting funds/ loans at an interest rate that will not exceed what you can afford.
- The home inspection should not reveal any major defects within the property.
- The seller should completely divulge any known problem with the property.
- The pest inspection should not show any major infestations or destruction to the property.
- The seller must complete any repairs that have been agreed on.

These contingencies must be gotten rid of in a process called *active proposal*. This is done by writing specific dates in your purchase offer. However, in some purchase agreements, contingencies depend on *passive approval* (constructive approval). This means that these contingencies are approved if you don't object to them by their specified deadlines. Buyers must understand the approval process and take the needed steps by the deadlines.

Meet the funding requirements

As a buyer, you are likely to deposit earnest money when you sign the purchase agreement. If the buyer backs out from buying the property, the earnest money will not be refunded by the seller as it would serve as their compensation. But if it is the seller who backs out, the money will be refunded to the buyer. To complete your purchase, pay some more money into escrow. This is because this earnest money is for the down payment, so you must get ready for other necessary payments before the deal gets closed. Failing to fund your escrow account can lead to the sale getting canceled and then the earnest money goes to the seller. Also, you could still be charged for the different services you used before the deal fell apart.

PS: Earnest money is the deposit a buyer pays to a seller to show their seriousness in buying a home. This deposit gives the buyer some extra time to get funds and run the title search, property appraisal, and inspections before closing.

1. **Get the loan approved:** Since underwriting can take a month or longer, your loan approval will come through at the end of the closing process. This is the last major piece of the puzzle that needs to fall into place for your closing to go on as you have scheduled.
2. **Final inspection:** Before you sign your closing papers, inspect the property one last time. This is to make sure that no damage has happened since your last home inspection. You should also make sure the seller has repaired all damages and that no additional damages have come up. Finally, check to see that nothing in the purchase agreement has been removed.

Paperwork

Paperwork is important when closing a property deal. No matter the stack of papers filled with complex legal terms, read all of them yourself. And if you understand nothing, this will be the time to hire a real estate attorney. Your agent can also prove helpful in making you understand complex legal terms. Now, even when you feel pressured by those waiting for you to sign your closing papers e.g. the mortgage lender or escrow agent still reads each page carefully and makes sure you understand as the signed papers can have a major impact for many years. Make sure the interest rate is correct, and all other agreed terms are stated accurately.

Below are some important documents you need to read carefully before signing. Also, note that there may slight differences in the documents based on the location where your property is and the type of property you are buying.

1. **Promissory note:** This is a legally binding commitment to repay your mortgage loan. It states the total amount you owe on your loan, the loan's interest rate, your monthly payment dates, the length of your loan, and acceptable payment methods. If you have an ARM (Adjustable Rate Mortgage) or variable-rate mortgage, your promissory note will detailedly explain how, when, and by how much your rate and payments are subject to change.
2. **Mortgage or deed of trust:** This is also known as the security instrument. It is a contract that gives your lender the right to seize your property through foreclosure if you cannot pay your mortgage as agreed. It restates the information in the promissory note, but also explains your rights and responsibilities as a homeowner and borrower, for instance, it will tell how you can occupy the property as a primary residence, or use it as a rental property, etc.) And outlines how and when your lender can seize your property.
3. **Initial escrow disclosure:** This document explains how your lender will distribute the money in your escrow account. It also has a breakdown of your principal-plus-interest and escrow payments, besides 12 months of expected monthly escrow balances. The escrow disclosure shows when and how much each escrow item (property taxes, insurance, and possibly PMI and HOA dues) is to be paid.
4. **Signature or name affidavit:** It is the signature that proves that the lender, loan servicer, government entities, and any other relevant parties, used to find out the legality of your signature on all closing documents. This is useful, especially during mortgage fraud investigations.
5. **Certificate of occupancy or occupancy statement:** If you are buying a new construction home, you will need to sign a certificate of occupancy stating that the home is ready and safe for occupants. Note that a missing certificate of occupancy can delay the closing process. When buying an existing home, you need to sign an occupancy statement that states the purpose of

the property, how soon you are expected to move in, and what will happen if you use the property for a purpose other than what was stated.

6. **First payment notification:** This document restates the amount (with an escrow, principal, and interest breakdown) and date of your first mortgage payment. It also includes information about how to make your payment, As well as the servicer's physical and web address.
7. **Seller or lender concessions:** This document shows the closing costs the seller and lender will pay if there are any.
8. **Servicing disclosure:** This document recognizes either the originating lender or a company that later purchases the mortgage. It also confirms your understanding that the loan can be transferred.
9. **Private mortgage insurance (PMI) disclosure:** If your loan-to-value ratio (LTV) is greater than 80%, your lender will probably ask for private mortgage insurance (PMI). This disclosure defines the PMI and describes your rights and responsibilities, including how and when it is paid (typically monthly, into the escrow account), and when you can ask that it should be stopped (typically after passing the 80% LTV threshold).
10. **Flood hazard statement:** This certifies that your property is or isn't in a special flood hazard zone. If your home is in a flood zone, it will probably need flood insurance.
11. **Appraisal acknowledgement:** This document confirms that you may collect a copy of your home's appraisal. It is often included in the mortgage application as well.
12. **Equal credit opportunity act disclosure:** This federally mandated form reinforces the fact that your loan cannot be denied based on any reason such as race or belief. It is also often stated in the mortgage application.
13. **Truth-in-lending disclosure:** This is another federally mandated document that explains the features of your mortgage loan, your monthly payments, and the total amount

(including principal and interest) you will be expected to pay throughout your loan.

14. **Mortgage fraud statements:** This document shows the different mortgage fraud, it lists potential penalties for people who are found guilty of mortgage fraud, and outlines the steps taken by the U.S. government to investigate and prosecute fraud suspects.
15. **Homeowners association covenants and agreements:** Contracts that apply to your membership in a homeowners' association sometimes appear during the closing. Although they are usually often sorted out before the closing day.
16. **Hazard disclosures:** Even though the purchase agreement naturally has all the hazard disclosures for your properties, you might still see the same disclosure or additional ones in your closing packet. Common disclosures cover things like the use of lead paint for homes built before 1978, radon, and subterranean wells.

Finally, compare your closing costs to the estimate you received at the beginning of the process and if you feel any fee is uncalled for, call it out.

Closing notice and disclosures

As soon as everything is in place for your closing, your title, escrow agent, or attorney is mandated to send you a formal **closing notice** with the time, date, taking part real estate agents (buyer's and seller's), and location of the closing. The location is usually the title or escrow agent's office, or the office of an attorney involved in the transaction. The notice also explains what you should come with closing event and they include the following:

- The presence of both buyers (if a married couple), or notarized power of attorney documentation that permits the present buyer to sign for the non-present one.
- Photo ID (passport or state-issued ID).
- List of your residences over the past 10 years.
- Ample funds to cover closing costs (usually a bank check or wire transfer).

Also, your title or escrow agent is mandated to send an official closing disclosure at least three business days before the closing date. Just like the loan estimate, the **closing disclosure** is a document that outlines all of your actual financial obligations related to the transaction: your closing costs, ongoing tax and insurance obligations, and a breakdown of your mortgage loan. It is written following the template of the loan estimate, even though it is more detailed and often has accounting line items or disclosures and caveats that were not in the loan estimate.

In conclusion, when you receive your closing disclosure, read through it carefully to ensure that the outlined obligations are like what is described in your loan estimate. Also, confirm that the terms of your mortgage loan are still as they should be, for instance, check that your interest rate or the rate structure has not changed from the loan estimate. If your closing costs differ significantly from the estimates or your mortgage loan is not what was originally stated, your lender or title or escrow agent could break the law. That is why it is a great idea to have an attorney throughout the closing process. It is also financially worthwhile to do so.

Closing Costs

Buyers are supposed to pay all closing costs when there are no other arrangements, but sometimes buyers and sellers agree to split the closing costs, especially in buyer's markets. This kind of agreement is outlined in the accepted purchase agreement and can be changed before the closing. Often, the buyer and seller do not have a specific agreement on who pays which closing costs. What they agree on a ratio e.g. the seller pays 45 percent while the buyer pays 55 percent or they can decide that one party pays a fixed sum of the closing cost and the other pays the rest.

Whichever way you bargain the closing costs, expect to pay the following costs when you close on a property. You may have to handle some of these costs on your own, for example, setting up a homeowner's insurance policy before the closing day. Also, depending on where your transaction takes place, your closing fees could probably differ from what I will explain. To accurately know how much you will be expected to pay, speak with a trusted and impartial real estate professional or attorney in your area.

Closing costs are paid through bank checks or wire transfers. A bank check is a better deal since they barely cost more than $1 or $2, while banks often charge $10 or more for a same-day wire transfer. If your title or escrow agent wants a wire transfer, ask them to send you the complete instructions (including receiving account number and bank routing number) with the closing notice.

1. **Home inspection and appraisal fee:** If you have not paid this fee upfront, they will be added to your closing costs. For these two services, expect to pay about $600 to $1,000.
2. **Loan origination and underwriting fees:** These fees cover the cost of your mortgage loan origination and underwriting services, but it does not cover the credit reports and other fees. Most origination fees are a percentage of the total purchase price, which ranges from 0.5 to 1.5 percent. These percentages are sometimes called *points*. For example, a 1 percent origination fee is equal to one point. Underwriting fees can also be charged as a percentage of the purchase price or a flat fee. In either case, it costs less than 1 percent of the home's purchase price. It is important to note that some mortgage loans that are called *no cost or no-fee loans*, don't have origination or underwriting fees. But these no-cost loans end up with higher interest rates than comparable traditional loans.
3. **Credit report fees:** Buyers usually have to pay for their lender's credit checks and reports which cost anything from $20 to $60, depending on how many credits reports the lender has to run and also with which credit reporting bureaus.
4. **Flood certification fee:** This is a small fee of about $20 that covers the cost of checking how close the location of the property you are buying is to local flood hazard areas. Flood

certification is necessary, especially if you will end up needing flood insurance. In some areas, you may be required to pay a one-time flood monitoring fee too, which costs between $25 and $50.

5. **First month's interest:** Many lenders ask for advance payment of the mortgage interest set to build up between the closing date and the date of the first mortgage payment. You should know that if you close on a property in the middle of the month, you most likely won't have to make a principal payment until the start of the next two months (that is if your payments are due on the first of the month). An example is when I closed on a house in May, but I didn't make my first principal payment until the first of July. But during the closing, I had to pay the interest set to accrue in May.
6. **Initial escrow deposit fee:** Lenders ask for an advance deposit into a secure escrow account to cover tax and insurance requirements set to build up between closing and their respective payment due dates. Practically, this means a buyer needs to pay in about a full year's worth of homeowner's insurance premiums (except they have already paid in advance) and also pay from 1 to 12 months of property tax premiums. Though property taxes are paid every six months, lenders are not willing to open a new escrow account with a balance barely enough to clear the first tax payment.
7. **Escrow buffer:** Many lenders tell buyers to pay an additional buffer to cover upward amendments to taxes and insurance premiums in the short-term, and to also reduce the chances of late payment, thus causing a negative escrow balance. The buffer's size depends on the monthly tax and insurance obligations.
8. **Homeowner's association (HOA) dues:** If you live in a community served by a homeowner's association, you must pay HOA dues monthly, annually, or biannually. Some lenders collate your dues into your escrow account and pay them on your behalf, the same as your taxes and insurance premiums.

If this is how it works for you, you might have to pay HOA dues by the end of the first mortgage period, which could be a year after the closing. Whether it is up to the lender or based on the HOA policy, HOA dues are not included in escrow and must be paid separately.

9. **Title or escrow services and insurance:** If bought, the cost of lender's and buyer's title insurance is packed into this class. An average of $1,000 should cover both policies, but then this fee varies largely because of the location and value of the property. This class also adds the cost of extra title work by the buyer's title company, escrow agent, or attorney, depending on their command, which also varies widely but is probably going to be higher if the buyer uses a licensed attorney. Finally, this class includes a settlement fee, which pays for the buyer's title or escrow agent's time on the closing day. This fee is between $200 to $400.
10. **Recording fee:** The city or county office tasked with recording real estate transfers in your area charges a fee for the work they do. This fee differs from one place to another and may also depend on the value or size of your property.
11. **Transfer taxes:** Your local and state governments probably charge transfer taxes on real estate transactions, based on the value of the property and possibly the parcel's zoning designation. The total state and local transfer taxes on residential real estate range between the high three-figure to mid-four-figure range.
12. **Broker fee:** Buyers' agents take their commission from the seller's proceeds, meaning that buyers do not pay them. The employers of the agents (realty groups or brokerages) often charge the buyer a relatively small service or referral fee. These can range from nominal sums ($100 or less) to $500 or more.

In summary, before you start the closing process, have a closing date in mind so you can work with the time and put your property on the market during the peak season. You remember the mistake I made about not putting the property I had close to a university during the peak rental season, right? That mistake happened because I didn't have a closing date from the outset.

Now that you have all this information, you will start your closing process with confidence since you know what you need to do.

Chapter Summary

In summary:

- Closing is signing the papers that make a property yours. But before the closing happens, there are a lot of things that need to be done. Whether you are buying your first property or buying a new property after selling the old one, you cannot move into your property or put it for rent until you officially close on the property (sign the papers).
- The closing day, which is the day you meet with the seller, your real estate agents, title or escrow agents, and other people involved in the transaction, is the day the property officially becomes yours. Because of the complexity of a real estate closing process, you might hire an attorney to help you out.
- Except you are buying a property with cash, get pre-approved for a mortgage before you even start looking for a property. Though being pre-approved is not a yardstick for closing a deal, most sellers just naturally expect property buyers to have a mortgage pre-approval letter. This is because having one can make the closing process quicker and even give you more bargaining power during negotiation.

In the next chapter, you will learn the after-closing details of a real estate investment.

6

AFTER CLOSING DETAILS

Having seen what you need and the cost of closing on a property, you need to ensure that your property is up and running. And if this means you need extra help, then why not?

Owning a rental property is a rewarding investment that brings in passive income monthly, which can help you prepare for early retirement. However, you need a good sense of business and management to make your real estate investment a success. Thus, you might need people who are experienced in the business to guide you.

Apart from getting the help of a property manager (which you have been enlightened about in a preceding chapter), you might need to get the help of an accountant, a real estate lawyer, and insurance services.

When buying a home, the seller goes into a written contract with a real estate agent. As soon as the agent finds a potential buyer, they start the negotiations and most times act as the middleman between the buyer and seller. Once the buyer and seller agree, they enter a formal written contract for the sale of the new property. This written contract is called the *purchase agreement*.

Buying the property follows the following summarised three steps:

1. The buyer gets a commitment to fund the purchase.
2. Then a title search is done to satisfy the lender and the buyer.
3. Finally, the seller hands over the property to the buyer, while the seller gets paid the purchase price as stated in the contract.

This process looks easy, but if there is no lawyer to guide you (the buyer) through this process, the result will not be a favorable one, especially if you end up signing the closing papers without a full understanding of the process.

A real estate lawyer is licensed to practice law and has their area of expertise to be real estate transactions. They are conversant with all aspects of the home purchase process and can represent buyers, sellers, or lenders. In areas where a lawyer needs to be present during a closing, that lawyer could be there just to represent the buyer's lender. In such as case, you need to get a lawyer for yourself if you want someone to speak about only your interests. Hiring a lawyer can cost from $200 to $300 an hour, or a flat fee of a couple of hundred dollars that are paid during closing.

A lawyer can help you avoid some common issues[1] associated with buying or selling a property. For instance, a seller may sign a brokerage agreement that does not include some legal issues. This is because realtors use standard forms with the belief that they will cover all situations. If there is no agreement, the seller may pay a brokerage commission even if there was no sale. Or the seller may be obligated to pay over one brokerage commission. Therefore, a property seller should have the counsel of a lawyer with a brokerage agreement. Even if the agreement is a standard form, its terms should be explained to the seller and improved, where necessary.

Even if you don't need a lawyer during the negotiation process, both you and the seller may want to consult with one to find answers to important legal questions like the tax consequences of the real estate transaction. The tax consequences are important to a property seller. For example, the income tax cost of a sale may be large if the seller makes a large profit. A lawyer can advise the seller whether they can take advantage of tax provisions that allow for the exclusion of capital gains in specific situations or not.

When do You Need to Hire a Lawyer

For purchase contract or agreement: The purchase agreement is the most significant document in the transaction. Even though standard printed forms can be used, a lawyer can help explain the forms, make adjustments and additions to show the desires of both the buyer and the seller.

Listed are issues that the lawyer may need to address in the purchase agreement:

- What if the property has been altered or what if there has been an addition to the property, was it done lawfully?
- If the buyer has plans to alter the property, can that be done lawfully?
- What happens if a buyer tells a home inspector to check the property and termites, asbestos, radon, or lead-based paint is found?
- What if the property contains hazardous waste?
- What are the legal outcomes if the closing does not take place, and what happens to the down payment?
- Will the down payment be held in an escrow account by a lawyer according to the escrow instructions? How will the payment be made? Is the closing dependent on the buyer getting funds?

Most buyers fund an ample portion of the purchase price for a property with a mortgage loan from a lending institution.

1. **During title search:** Once the purchase agreement is signed, it is vital to find the state of the seller's title to the property to

satisfy both the buyer and the financial institution. Normally, a title search is ordered from an abstract or title insurance company. However, in some states, title insurance is not standard. In such a situation, a lawyer should go through the status of title and state if there is a lien on the property. The title search does not tell the buyer or seller anything about existing and prospective zoning (this is the government's way of allocating what areas should be used for residential buildings, industries, etc). But a lawyer can say whether zoning prohibits a two-family home, or whether planned developments violate zoning laws. In addition, a lawyer can show the restrictions forced by a previous owner, and whether any legal restrictions will prevent you from being able to sell the property.

2. **During closing:** Closing on a property is the most important aspect of the purchase and sale transaction, and this usually involves dozens of pages of legal documents to go through. A closing statement should be ready before the closing, and it should state the debits and credits to the buyer and seller, respectively. A lawyer can help both the seller and buyer go through the review, which can intimidate and confuse a first-time homebuyer. During the closing, title passes from seller to buyer, who pays the balance of the purchase price, which is paid in part from the proceeds of a mortgage loan. Once the deed and other closing documents are signed, the lawyer makes sure these documents are correctly implemented and explained to everyone.

3. **In uncommon scenarios:** Below are some uncommon scenarios where you will need a legal expert's advice concerning your property:

- When you are buying a property that is part of a special type of sale, e.g. as an estate sale, quick sale, auction, or purchase from a bank.
- When you are buying a property in another state.

- When you are selling a property, that is the major part of a divorce settlement.
- When you are selling a property that was owned by a family member and you are now in charge of the estate.
- When you are buying or selling a property that has major issues like structural damage.
- When you have a serious money problem and you are trying to sell a property with liens (a lien is a claim or legal right against assets that collateral to pay back a debt) it.

How to Find a Real Estate Lawyer

You can get recommendations from real estate agents and lenders who you trust. You can also search for real estate lawyers in your area, look up the local American Bar Association chapter, or contact a non-profit organization that helps homeowners. Finally, interview a few lawyers so you can compare their approach, rates, and availability, then pick the best fit.

These are some questions you can ask the lawyers you interview:

1. **Do you charge by the hour or you charge a flat fee?** You should out what the price range is and if the fee includes the time to review, discuss and even negotiate aspects of all documents or if it is just to attend the closing.
2. **How available will you be during the process?** You need to be sure of their availability, especially when you are in the middle of a negotiation that might become a debate and needs to be resolved quickly. It is only natural for you to want your lawyer to be available in such a situation so they can advise you and negotiate with the other party.
3. **How many residential real estate transactions do you advise on each year?** This question can give you an idea of the lawyer's experience with real estate transactions. It will also help you know if the lawyer is a rookie, a highly demanded

one, or even too busy to give one-on-one attention or be available for negotiations.
4. **How are you involved in real estate transactions?** Real estate transactions can be versatile, so it's important to get a lawyer who is experienced in the type of help you need.

Advantages of hiring a real estate lawyer:

- **Exclusive representation:** When you are buying a property, everyone involved wants to get the deal done. This can make you feel you are on your own sometimes. However, if you hire a lawyer, you will have access to an independent third-party expert who can go over the contract with you, explain things where you are not clear, and represent your best interests throughout the transaction.
- **Hiring a real estate lawyer helps you uncover the unresolved issues with buying a property:** If a real estate lawyer's fee is within your means, hiring one could be a significant investment. This is because when a major issue that has not been negotiated is uncovered, it can cost you thousands of dollars or more to sort out. Sometimes, it might just be unfixable.
- **Peace of mind:** Even if you don't want to hire a lawyer for when you are buying your property, you might feel better knowing someone is there to explain complex legal terms or issues. A real estate lawyer can also reassure you are making the right decisions in the buying process.

Disadvantages of hiring a real estate lawyer:

- **It could become a hassle:** If your lawyer finds reasons to bump heads with the other party, for example, making a big deal about something minor, it might delay the closing and

could be costly if the fight continues and you have to pay them by the hour.
- **The cost:** If you have quite a straightforward transaction and a real estate lawyer is not needed in your state, just stick with the real estate agent and title company helping you with the purchase of the property. The money you could have used to pay an attorney can be saved to go for the down payment or other necessities.

Whether you decide to hire a real estate lawyer or not will depend on your preference and ability to pay a little more at your closing. But, if you can have a team of professionals on your side: a real estate representative, lender, inspector, and lawyer, it should make the property-buying experience smoother, especially if you are a newbie investor.

Getting Insurance for Your Real Estate Property

Insuring your home is not the same as insuring a rental property. Since a homeowner's insurance policy differs from a landlord insurance policy, as a landlord, you will need to do some findings and choose the one that meets your needs the most. When valuing your property, do it at full replacement cost and not the actual cash value. Real cash value policies remove 15 years of depreciation instead of paying the current costs for materials and labor.

As a rental property owner, a landlord insurance policy may suit your needs better. This insurance helps protect your investment by providing coverage for:

1. **Property damage:** This covers damages on the property caused by tenants and fire, storms, vandalism, and theft.
2. **Liability:** This pays legal costs and medical bills for tenants or visitors who get injured while on your property.
3. **Loss of income:** This compensates you for lost rent if your tenants have to leave your property because.

Besides your landlord's insurance, you could make it mandatory for your tenants to have renter's insurance. This is a reasonably priced policy that covers them for circumstances your insurance won't cover, thus minimizing the possibility of them trying to hold you accountable.

Renter's insurance allows your tenants to:

1. Repair or replace any property that gets damaged by fire, vandalism, or theft.
2. Cover injuries or any harm is done to their visitors (they can also pay legal costs and pay medical bills).

Insurance policies are written to guide the insurance coverage. This means that for damage to be covered, it must be sudden and accidental. With a slow leak that caused damage over many months, it is not sudden or accidental, so it will not be covered by insurance. Another example is, assuming your roof shatters from old age, and not from the effect of a heavy storm, it will probably not be covered by insurance.

Conclusively, some insurance companies give mind-boggling rates for their policies. Here's the thing, if the company is not well-known and its rates are too good to be true, this should be a warning sign. Find out the company's reputation instead of believing the salesperson's words hook, line and sinker. Critically study their insurance policy, see what it covers and what it doesn't. In doing this, you may find out that what you thought was enough insurance coverage is hardly the legal minimum in your area. Also, when looking for the benefits of property insurance, insist on quality coverage. Remember, that cheap insurance can end up being costly in the long run.

Hiring an Accountant for Your Real Estate Property

[2]Because we say real estate investment is a way to earn passively, there is active work involved in a lot of ways. As a real estate investor, you know that you will have to put in many hours, effort, and knowledge into running a successful real estate business. However, you cannot do everything by yourself (even if you want to). Just as it is good to hire a property manager, a real estate lawyer and get an insurance policy for your real estate investment, it will also help you hire a competent

accountant who will handle your tax returns and maintain your account records effectively for the following reasons:

You are not a tax expert

Taxation and accounting are very broad. Accountants spend lots of money and train for years to get skilled. They even still pay for continuous learning that keeps them up to date on the latest tax code changes. An investor might have read one or two books on tax planning, so they assume they can do anything related to tax and accounting. However, the truth remains that they are not qualified to be a tax expert, neither should they attempt to become one. Instead, investors should do the following:

- Hire a skilled accountant to take care of the taxation aspects of their real estate business.
- Learn about taxes and accounting so they can understand what their accountant does and know how to read and interpret financial reports.
- Focus on buying more property, and managing existing investments more profitable.

1. **Accounting software is just not enough:** When people think cheap tax software is all they need to file a tax return, it bewilders me! I will not condemn tax software because they still function well and deliver excellent results for people with regular jobs or a few stock or mutual fund investments. The reason is simply that their tax returns are straightforward. But on the contrary, when you own an investment property, the complexity of filing tax returns switches up to the max! Software lacks specific data for your unique situation. An instance would be when you plan to sell a property in a few years and an accountant helps you plan or when you can foresee that you will make a lot of revenue this year, but little next year and an accountant helps you sort out and reduce the

taxes paid across both years. All these things an accountant can do for you, the software cannot.
2. **DIY is costly:** I remember the story of an investor who had many rental properties and had been doing his tax returns for the last three years. When he finally hired an accountant owing to his increased workload, the accountant discovered from his returns that his client (the investor) had neglected half of his property expenses, which caused him to pay more taxes than he should have for each of his properties every year he remained the landlord. Luckily, the investor could adjust the previous tax returns. But let's assume he never hired an accountant to help him with his taxes, he would have continued to pay more taxes than he should.

Other benefits of hiring an accountant include:

1. They help you find and take advantage of as many tax benefits as possible.
2. They follow the rules and regulations of accounting's changing tax code.
3. They help you keep track of your business transactions.
4. They help you stay organized by using efficient accounting or record-keeping systems.

How to Hire a Competent Accountant

Although you need an accountant to help you maximize profit in your real estate business, be careful not to hire an incompetent one. Some accountants are disorganized and will cause more mess than you expected, hence the need to hire a sound accountant. Hiring a competent account should be like any interview process you will conduct for an expert whose services you need. The following questions will be helpful to you during your interview with a potential accountant.

1. What types of businesses do you normally work with?

2. Do you have a specialty in any area of business accounting?
3. How many of your clients have a similar structure to my business? (NB: explain how your business operates so they can answer this satisfactorily).
4. Are you a stand-alone business, or do you work for a larger public accounting firm?
5. Are you a licensed CPA (Certified Public Accountant)?
6. Do you have any other certification that will prompt me to hire you? (NB: Being a certified public accountant is a plus and not a must especially for their job description).
7. What kinds of services can you provide for me (for example, quickbooks, tax returns, tax planning, tax advice, or any other service)?
8. How many years of accounting experience do you have?
9. Do you have any investment properties yourself? If so, what type do you own (are they rental properties, vacation homes, farmland, properties you have sold on land contract, etc.)?
10. How much capacity can you currently put in for some additional?
11. Would any other person under your employ be handling my books beside you? If so, what is their level of expertise in real estate accounting and how much supervision will you have over them?
12. What kinds of things will you request from me to carry out your job effectively?
13. What is your service charge based on my job description for you)? Do you charge hourly, weekly, monthly or annually?
14. Are there any methods you can implement to help me save money on taxes?
15. Do I need to sign a contract/agreement if we decide to work together? If so, can I review it before it expires?
16. Can you give me any work references? (NB: Some accountants may not give you any references, as it may breach their confidentiality contract with their clients. So if they cannot give you any reference, it shouldn't stop them from getting the

job if they are qualified. Nevertheless, there is no harm in asking just in case they can give you one or two references).

Based on the answers you get from the above-listed questions, you can expand the conversation even further to get more insight into your potential hire. All the same, these questions are powerful indicators of whether you are about to hire a competent real estate accountant.

A good accountant responds quickly (usually within 48 hours or less) no matter if you reached out to them through phone or email. If they cannot respond within a day or two, do not respond at all, or if they respond in a manner that does not answer your questions, hire someone else. If they cannot impress you in the initial stage of their work, they will probably cannot do better even when you continue working with them.

Also, as human beings, we will naturally show favor to the people we like but keep in mind that hiring a competent person (someone with the right experience and know-how) to do the job your business needs is the priority and not how you like them. Your aim with conducting the interview is to discover their competence and after all has been said, an accountant's skills and attention to detail has little to do with their personality. Therefore, ensure you choose the candidate who comes across as the best qualified.

If you are still considering if hire an accountant, know that the cost is nothing compared to the savings you will have from not making costly mistakes, the calmness when you know that your tax returns are done well and that you are also maximizing your tax savings.

What Your Property Management Team Needs to Get the Cash Flow From Your Rental Property Coming In

There is a famous saying that goes, *"No man is an island."* The same also applies to your real estate investment business. If you must succeed in it, you need certain people called **team members to** help you achieve your goals. A team can either make or break your real estate investment business. Therefore, this implies that you must have a strong team if you want to have a profitable real estate investment business.

Your real estate property management team comprises the following people:

1. A property manager.
2. A leasing agent.
3. An accountant.
4. Maintenance officer.
5. Marketing officer.

A profitable investment property brings in monthly cash flow, which is about 1 percent of the property's purchase price. However, an investment property cannot automatically bring in cash if no work is done. To make sure you get cash flow from your investment property, you must:

1. **Set the right price for your rent:** When you fix the right price for your property, it will be easy for it to be found in online search results, you will generate more inquiries and showings and tenants will say yes to renting your property at the drop of a hat. Apart from the 1 percent rule, you can get an estimate of what your rent should be by putting yourself in the tenant's shoes and by checking local rental listings to see what your competitors charge. When you predict the monthly fixed costs such as the estimated cost of repairs/maintenance, taxes, insurance, and homeowners' association fees, you will fix a rent price that ensures you still make a profit at the end of every month. If in the long run, you decide to increase your rent, do not be greedy but make sure it is in line with the current market rental rates. Also, inform your tenants a minimum of 90 days about this new change and don't increase the rent more than once in two years.

2. **Choose your tenants carefully:** there is nothing as horrible as having an investment property with the potential to do well, and then it becomes crippled because of bad tenants. Before you rent your property to anyone, they must be thoroughly screened. To screen potential tenants, ask for the following:

- Their employment history and income.
- Their rental history.
- Credit information.
- References or referees.

To make sure your rent comes in as it should, you should not allow late payments or permit any lease violation, and ask tenants for regular feedback so you can improve where there is a need. And when you eventually find good tenants, treat them well and do what you can to make them long-term.

1. **Focus on long-term opportunities:** Long-term tenants mean you are certain of consistent cash flow. Because a long-term renter pays the same rental fee every month, it's naturally more stable and less stressful than renting to short-stay tenants or vacationers. Even though short-term tenants are awesome during the high rental period, if you want consistent year-round income, long-term is the better pick.
2. **Know a little something about taxes:** As I stated earlier, even when you have an accountant in your team, take the time to study and know a few things about tax and tax returns as it will help you understand and appreciate the work your accountant does. Knowing something about taxes will help you take advantage of the tax benefits available to you.
3. **Keep the correct records:** Having organized records makes it easy for an investor to get data and manage their property. If your records are correct, you will never be caught unaware by a lease termination, vacancy, or unexpected tax bill. Whether you use a basic spreadsheet or fancy CRM (Customer

Relationship Management) software, just make sure you use a system that is easy to access, track and update. Lastly, excellent record keeping makes it much easier to get through tax season.
4. **Look for quality maintenance workers that are also cheap to work with:** Whenever there is a need for either major or minor repairs to be done on your property, contract the job to contractors who will do a phenomenal job at an affordable fee. This is where the advantage of having a property manager comes to play, as they have good relationships with many contractors they have established a working relationship with, who will give discounts. Another awesome trick to minimizing repair costs is by getting insurance for your property and even appliances.

Each of your team members should carry out their duties effectively so their effort will count for something in the overall success of your investment. As it is, you are the leader of your team and decide where you steer the ship even as you get professional advice from the rest of your team members.

Finally, encourage openness and communication within your team and to you. If one team member knows something that will be helpful to another team member, when there is openness, they can offer their advice. Again, no man is an island, and to get far in life, you need people.

Chapter Summary

In summary:

- As soon as the agent finds a potential buyer, they start the negotiations and most times act as the middleman between the buyer and seller. Once the buyer and seller agree, they enter a formal written contract for the sale of the new property. This written contract is called the *purchase agreement*.

- Owning a rental property is a rewarding investment that brings in passive income monthly, which can help you prepare for early retirement. However, you need a good sense of business and management to make your real estate investment a success. Thus, you might need people who are experienced in the business to guide you.
- Even if you don't want to hire a lawyer when you are buying your property, you might feel better knowing someone is there to explain complex legal terms or issues. A real estate lawyer can also reassure you are making the right decisions in the buying process.

In the next chapter, you will learn about the partnership opportunity with a team of seasoned real estate investors.

7

PARTNERSHIP OPPORTUNITY WITH A TEAM OF SEASONED REAL ESTATE INVESTORS

When I found out ninety percent of millionaires made their money through real estate, it opened my eyes to the possibility of attaining financial freedom, so I jumped right in. I bought a townhome in 2013, rehabbed the property, and rented it out. After having to repair walls, plumbing, electrical problems, and other damages, I was burned out. The property was making substantial money that was enough for my wife, three sons, and I to live in northern New York while none of us worked.

Even though it was good money, I lost some much time which made me sell the property. Selling the property was great for my family. I found a real estate investor, Kris Khron[1], out in Utah and I knew I had to meet him. After I met and talked with Kris, I was down with partnering with him as he and his team have done over $1 billion in real estate. Which meant they were doing something right.

We came up with a finance game plan for my needs. Since then, every year from the start of our partnership to date, I have doubled my income. Also, the time I had lost in running my first rental property business, working with Kris has given me that time back.

An amazing thing about partnering with Kris and his team is that they do all the work for you. Kris finds the deals, manages the rehabilitation, finds the tenants, works with the property managers, sets up the LLC to protect us (his partners). He took care of everything I didn't want to get involved with.

Like many others who have tangible testimonials to share, I am also a part of a program where we partner with people who are interested in getting into the game of real estate investment. This partnership is a hands-off process that works in two ways:

1. Those who do not have the time to get into real estate investing.
2. Those who need an experienced mentor or someone to guide them into a successful real estate investment business.

Kris Khron is a business coach, best-selling author, world-class speaker, and life-changing breakthrough mentor. For over a decade now, Kris has helped people grow their wealth, health, and personal power. Through his ground-breaking methods of investing in real estate and his limitless belief breakthrough, he helps people bridge the gap between where they are and the results they want (the results of their potential demands). Before creating his unique life experiences, Kris mentored thousands of people in creating, managing, protecting, and growing wealth through novel real estate investment and other strategies. He is an expert wealth coach with his greatest expertise found in real estate.

Kris has five strategies for building wealth using real estate without having to use your own money or credit by teaching the following:

1. How to cash-free real estate.
2. How to get 100 percent bank financing for your deals.
3. How to do high-profit commercial real estate.
4. How to double the value of a property in 30 days.
5. How to cash in on inflation and minimize taxes.

If you would like to know more about Kris Khron, his team, how he partners with people to help them invest profitably in real estate with an ROI of 20 percent. If you would also like to read the testimonials of people who have benefited from their partnership with him or if you want to get started investing in real estate by partnering with Kris and his team, then email me at me at mr.williams@ejwilliamsinvesting.com and please put "Partnering Opportunity" into the email subject line. Talk to you soon.

CONCLUSION

It is not impossible to retire early using property investment[1]. Real estate investment is one of the best ways to become financially free and have an early retirement. You must also know there are many ways or methods to retire by investing in real estate.

These methods work for different people, no matter how different their methods of investing are. And they are:

- **Through positive rental properties:** With this method, you buy a property, and right from the first day; it brings in more money in rental income than the expenses you paid for. This is an instant way to increase your passive income and get closer to early retirement. Even if the rent doesn't increase with time (which is rarely possible) you can still retire early by simply buying more positive cash flow properties. Also, after a while, your rental income will increase and you will pay your mortgage. So your total positive cash flow can pay for your lifestyle using a few properties.
- **Through buy and hold for rental income:** This method is like

CONCLUSION

a positive rental property. However, when you buy the property, it is negatively geared and costs you money. This is done to secure a quality property with good potential capital gains. The next thing to do is to allow the rental income to increase and eventually cover the mortgage expenses and your property becomes positively cash flowed. Over time, you can take advantage of your equity to invest in more properties and expand your portfolio. But remember, the end goal is to live off rental income. Often people who use this method will sell some properties to pay off debts on their other properties and then live off the cash flow.

- **Through buy and hold for capital gains:** This is the process whereby you buy a property just for the capital gains (which is the profit gotten from an investment or the sale of a property). Then you rent the property out, but they still cost you some money every month. The essence of doing this is for the value of the property to double every 7-10 years. As long as your property continues to go up in value, have enough equity to live off indefinitely. However, depending on banks to lend you money and the fact that it is difficult to find funds after retirement should make you research this strategy carefully before you decide to use this method. Alternatively, you can sell your properties to get the capital gains, but then you have to pay capital gains tax and you will lose all future growth.
- **Through buy, renovate, and sell:** With this method, you buy a property that needs to be fixed and then you sell it for more than the cost price of the property and your renovation expenses combined. Say, for instance, you buy a property for $50,000 and you spend $20,000 on renovations. To say you have been successful with this buy, renovate and sell method, you must have sold the renovated property for an amount greater than $70,000. If you can pull off this strategy well, it is a great way to make ample cash that can help you retire early. However, be mindful that if this method turns you into a

CONCLUSION

handyperson who is constantly fixing properties, then you are not retiring.
- **Through buy, add value, hold and then sell:** This is the process whereby you buy a property and then increase the value by renovating it immediately. Doing this will probably add value to the rental income, or it may increase the market value of the property or both. Once the renovations are done, you hold the property. You can take advantage of the equity in the property by reinvesting it, or you can use the increased rental yield to start a positive cash flow property.
- **Through buy, hold and sell:** This method has to do with buying a property, holding onto it for some time, and then selling it to get the capital gains on the property. It is a general occurrence that almost all properties go up in value. Therefore, by holding onto the property you get to take advantage of market growth, which you will later get when you sell the property. The cash profit you make from the sale of the property can be put into a low-risk investment which will yield low interest or saved towards another investment property that can hasten your early retirement plan.

Whichever one (or maybe more) of the above methods you choose to adopt for your early retirement plan, make sure it is well-aligned with your values

In reading this book, you have learned:

1. That limiting beliefs are not facts but result from what we were told as kids, the environment we grew up in and the experience we have had in life. These limiting beliefs are also the reason many do not go after their goals.
2. There are 5 steps to owning your first rental property and they include: *choosing the right funding option, finding the right property, finding a property manager, closing on the property, and the after closing details.*

CONCLUSION

3. That there are many funding options to help you get your first rental property. Those funding options are *loans, partnering, hard money lender, 401K, IRA, Wholelife insurance, and TSP.*
4. That finding the right property starts with writing all you want in your rental property after which you can screen out those properties that are not the right fit by using the amount of cash flow per month (which is usually 1 percent of the property's purchase price).
5. That hiring a property manager to oversee the affairs of your rental property is a smart investment as it will take your mind off the challenges involved with running a rental property business. With a property manager handling your rental property, you will have the time to focus on more important things like acquiring more investment properties while they bring in more tenants.
6. That closing on a property is the most important aspect of buying your rental property. It is also important to have a real estate lawyer that will guide you through the difficult legal terms in a closing document and help with the negotiation. It is also important for you to have a closing date in mind, give yourself enough time for the closing and get a pre-approved mortgage.
7. That it is important to have a team of experts who will work with you to help make your real estate investment business a success. This team of experts includes, but is not limited to, only *property manager, real estate lawyer, maintenance officer, marketing officer, accountant and leasing agent.* Also, getting insurance for your rental property is an important step that helps minimize repair costs so you can maximize profit.

Now that you've gotten acquainted with the nitty-gritty of how to get your first rental property, I cannot wait to see you put this knowledge to work. I would also love to hear your thoughts on how helpful this book was to you.

CONCLUSION

Tell me your experience with buying your first rental property in the review box. I look forward to hearing from you.

NOTES

2. Funding Options

1. https://www.investopedia.com/best-investment-property-loans-5079478
2. https://loans.usnews.com/reviews/quickenloans-mortgage
3. https://www.consumersadvocate.org/va-loans/c/veterans-united-va-loans-review
4. https://www.nerdwallet.com/reviews/mortgages/citimortgage
5. https://www.merchantmaverick.com/reviews/lendio-review/
6. https://www.nerdwallet.com/reviews/mortgages/northpointe-bank-mortgage
7. https://www.lendingtree.com/reviews/mortgage/nationwide-home-lending/32529505
8. https://www.creditsuite.com/blog/lending-one-review/
9. https://www.thebalance.com/hard-money-basics-315413
10. https://www.fool.com/millionacres/real-estate-financing/can-you-use-your-401k-make-real-estate-investments/
11. https://www.tsp.gov

3. Find the Right Property

1. https://thefinancebff.com/6-things-you-need-to-know-before-buying-your-first-investment-property/
2. https://www.investopedia.com/articles/mortgages-real-estate/08/buy-rental-property.asp
3. https://thesmartmoneylife.com/top-10-features-of-a-profitable-rental-property/

4. Find a Property Manager

1. https://learn.rootstock.com/blog/how-to-choose-a-property-manager
2. https://www.bricksandagent.com/blog/benefits-of-using-property-management-company

5. Close on the Property

1. https://www.moneycrashers.com/house-closing-process-documents/
2. https://www.investopedia.com/articles/mortgages-real-estate/10/closing-home-process.asp

NOTES

6. After Closing Details

1. https://www.findlaw.com/realestate/buying-a-home/why-you-need-a-lawyer-when-you-buy-or-sell-a-house.html
2. https://www.spirepoint.com/top-5-reasons-to-use-an-accountant-for-real-estate/

7. Partnership Opportunity With a Team of Seasoned Real Estate Investors

1. https://www.kriskrohn.com/learn-about-kris-a

Conclusion

1. https://onproperty.com.au/retire-early-through-property-investment/

www.ingramcontent.com/pod-product-compliance
Lightning Source LLC
Chambersburg PA
CBHW020911080526
44589CB00011B/540